WHY NOT HAVE IT ALL

A Spiritual Guide to Balance and Fulfillment

MRS. BONITA ANDREA SHELBY

◆ FriesenPress

Suite 300 - 990 Fort St
Victoria, BC, V8V 3K2
Canada

www.friesenpress.com

Foreword by: Pastor Don WIlliam Shelby Jr.
Photography: Patricia Gray McDowell
Graphic Design- Book Cover - Farrah
Scripture References -The Bible- Kings James Version
Bishop Don W. Shelby Jr- Ministries
+Google Resources -Women really Talk More Than Men http://www.dailymail.co.uk/sciencetech/
article-2281891/Women-really-talk-men-13-000-words-day-precise.html#ixzz4aq5aYduE

ISBN
978-1-4602-9571-7 (Hardcover)
978-1-4602-9572-4 (Paperback)
978-1-4602-9573-1 (eBook)

1. RELIGION, CHRISTIAN LIFE, INSPIRATIONAL

Distributed to the trade by The Ingram Book Company

Table of Contents

14

15

16

17

FOREWORD BY BISHOP DON WILLIAM SHELBY JR.

First of all, I celebrate my "wife for Life", Bonita Andrea Shelby on the long-awaited release of her first book, "Why Not Have It All." Preachers of Detroit provided a platform to introduce Bonita to the world as a woman who loves God, loves her husband, and loves her family while succeeding in business and ministry. I am excited that her recipe for balance and success will now be released to the world. This is a masterpiece and literature that has not just been well written but also well lived. Bonita, is a living witness that you can be comfortable in your own skin and reach heights that will bring personal fulfillment and growth. Whether you are married, single, businessperson, or just someone trying to bring order to your life this book is for you!

FOREWORD BY DR. MEDINA PULLINGS

Overflows! Overflowing peace, joy, love, wealth, health, contentment, and more! Never settle for less! Absolutely receive of the bountiful supply that never runs dry! God's best and nothing less because truly through Jesus Christ, you really can have it all! Passionately pursue your dreams while keeping Jesus at the center of it all! This is what immediately comes to mind when describing live life on purpose! Maximizing every moment! To live life to the fullest is the core theme of Lady Bonita's inspiring book, "Why not have it all?"

"Why not have it all" causes one to look within and ask the question that only one's self can answer. Essentially, taking a deeper look at what it truly means to having it all. Envisioning what that entails, Lady Bonita provides the practical tools needed to achieve this goal. I believe Lady Bonita's book will lead many into authentic fulfillment. This book serves as a refresher of what truly is possible and made available through Jesus Christ!

One thing people know that are fortunate enough to know Lady Bonita personally is that she has a GINORMOUS heart for people. I am not surprised that she would pen such a manuscript of hope, inner reflection, true life's happiness, and peace, equipping the reader to live a healthy, fulfilled, balanced life! I get excited just talking about it! Reading this book highlights what is absolutely essential to having it all! Be sure to share a copy with a friend!

Medina Pullings

Pastor, United Nations Church Int'l

ACKNOWLEDGEMENTS

BISHOP DON WILLIAM SHELBY JR.

Foremost I would like to acknowledge my Lord and Savior Jesus Christ for his love shown towards me and my family. I am thankful for the opportunity to minister to others through writing and sharing my life experiences. All honor, praise and glory is given to God who has strategically ordained my purpose. This book is dedicated to God and the infinite wisdom and knowledge that is shared daily.

To my best friend in the entire world Bishop Don W. Shelby Jr. my hubby, soul-mate, and my everything. I thank God for my husband who is my Pastor, mentor. The day we met and to date, Don pours into my life and gives me the desire to be my absolute best. Every endeavor and dream that I have shared with Donny, he has consistently encouraged me to move forward and strategize plans to make my dreams a reality. Thank you Don for protecting me and being a great father to our children. Thank you for being a wonderful provider and every day that I spend with you, I love you more. I can remember your patience with me down through the years. I can remember when we married I had never washed clothes because my mother always washed until the day I married. The first few months of washing loads was a disaster...

everything was pink including your t-shirts, white dress shirts and underwear. I can see the look on your face, although you were disappointed, you looked at me with such love and said come on I'm going to show you how to separate clothes and wash. You did just that and now I am a pro... I can separate and wash clothes effortlessly! That's the love you have exemplified throughout our 29 years of marriage and I'm thankful. I appreciate your example of loving others unconditionally and the awesome word and revelation that comes forth from your mouth. Your faith and tenacity are evident as we walk through life together. Don you are a "go getter" and you never allow the word "quit" to be a part of your vocabulary. I always say that I am your biggest fan, cheerleader and student of the word. I have many notes from bible study and when faced with difficult decisions, I can reference the words that you speak. I can remember some of the toughest situations that I had to reach back and remember your wisdom much of this book represents some of those words. My life changed when God called you to Pastor and as the first member of Burning Bush International, I want to be the first to say, "thank you". You never leave me behind but you always have a desire to stay close and have me near your side. I don't take that for granted. You make me feel like a princess, diva, and "a lady" because you are such a gentleman. Donny you are my rock, strong.... resilient and a man after God's heart. I love doing life with you Donny and couldn't imagine my life without you.

MY CHILDREN

To my children, Don William Shelby III (D3), Courtney Lucille Shelby, Andrea Paige Shelby, Trenton Blake Shelby, and Amber Lauren-Seth Shelby, known as......." The Shelby 5"! I appreciate all of you as my "special gifts" from God and I cherish being your mother. I love the way that you love God and work in ministry. Each Sunday I witness all of you waking up, getting up out of the house and heading to the church to offer your God given "spectacular" talents to Burning Bush International Ministries. Mommy loves you dearly as unique individuals destined to be great! I can name so many instances that you poured into my life even as babies. Now that you are all adults you continue to pour using all of your talents and gifts to help your parents. You have such a pure heart towards ministry and I know that God has great things in store for each of your lives. I am thankful for children who are intelligent and in pursuit of academic excellence. Always remember there are supernatural miracles on the horizon for you collectively and individually. My desire is that you would continue to reverence God in all that you do and love each other unconditionally. When one wins, we all win. Shelby 5, you are winners and you are winning!

DAD AND MOM

To my Dad and Mom. Dad and Mom thank you for your continued love and the way in which you provided and cared for all of my siblings.

DAD

Daddy (Marvin Earl Tooson) thank you and I know that I will always be your baby girl! You always came through with every request in my childhood from putting coats and clothes on hold and the faith that I had that my daddy would get it for me without a dime in my pocket. I am tickled at the fact that I would tell you (before you worked your midnight shift) that I expected that you would leave my money on the dresser (for my clothes) before you went to work. Indeed, the money was there. Thank you Daddy for being a great example of a strong man, father and mentor.

MOM

Mommy, (Lucille Virginia Tooson) a whole lot of this book is dedicated to you, my "she-ro". I have learned so much from you and I thank god for your obedience to give God your life and then in turn you raised all of us in the church and taught us well. I learned about missions and evangelism from you. I can remember as a teenager that you would drive me to church meetings to speak at youth programs and represent our district. You took time to help me prepare inspirational words and then you were at every school event that I can remember. Thank you for all of the full course dinners every day, breakfast every morning, putting me on the bus every day and then going to work. Thank you for arranging my care and making sure that I never suffered for anything. You and dad have always said that if we (your children) are happy... you are happy. Well, I want to let you and dad know that I am happy! I love you both!

MOM 2

To my Mom (Mother Lucille Shelby), you are my heart, I thank God that when I met Donny and he introduced you for the first time, I fell in love with you. I appreciate that you love and care for me as your blood daughter. I have never considered myself a "daughter-in-law", but your daughter. You are an answer to my prayers and the fact that the Lord gave me another mom named "*Lucille*", I know that's not by coincidence, but it is the will of God. I cherish you Mom and thanks for giving me such a wonderful, God-fearing and loving son (Donny).

IN HONOR OF DAD, DON WILLIAM SHELBY, JR.

I want to dedicate this book to the memory of my other "Father in love" who is deceased, Don William Shelby Sr. He was quietly powerful and he always showed true and genuine love. My name was affectionately, "Nita." You are missed, and I will never forget you and your quiet loving demeanor.

MY SIBLINGS

My oldest brother Marvin Jr. (Deceased), I love you although I never met you.... I would spend countless hours looking at your picture on mom's dresser and thinking about you. Even now I think about the great impact you would have made on this world as my big brother.

Sharolyn, my oldest sister, thank you of all the outfits and sending me to high school every Friday after you got paid with a new outfit. My "best dressed" award in my junior/senior year was in honor of you!

Narvin-my "bubby", thanks for taking such good care of me. When I started kindergarten and had to ride the bus to school, because you knew that most of my school days would be spent alone due to the age differences of my siblings... You took great care of me in the one year that we were together. We rode the same bus and you would keep me close on the seat next to you every day. You made sure that I had everything that I needed. You made sure that my hair was in place and I was neat getting off the bus and you dared *anybody* to touch me. I was your little sister *baby doll*. I remember getting off the bus and you (my big brother), walking me to class and letting my teacher know that if I needed anything to come and get you out of class. You would take my coat off, hang it up and then walk me to my desk every day. Not only that, although I was in class a half day you would come back at least 3 times a day knock on the door and peek in to see if I was alright. Thanks big brother. I love you.

Marvetta, my big sister that always played dolls with me. When I couldn't find anyone else to play with you were always willing and patient. My oldest sister was outside with her high school friends and they would "fake" me out and say, "Go back to the house and look under the bed for a present that they hid for me.... they wanted to get rid of the little sister, after I went to the house and came back complaining and crying you would always say, let's go play dolls. Thanks Vette, Vette! That time with you made it ALL better!

To my nieces, nephews and my sister and brothers "in-love," I appreciate and love all of you!

BURNING BUSH INTERNATIONAL MINISTRIES FAMILY

To my Church family, Burning Bush International Ministries...Ypsilanti, Jackson and Pontiac, Michigan. Thank you for loving the Shelby family! Pastor and I are grateful to have been entrusted with such an awesome congregation (church family). As a Pastor's wife, I can honestly say that all of you have blessed me tremendously down through the years and I appreciate that you have not caused me heartache. I am privileged to serve as your Pastor's wife/spiritual mom. I often think about the pain and headache that so many congregations have caused their Pastor's wife... but I can honestly say that I have not felt that pain. Through ups and downs, or any difficulties you never cease to amaze me. I love all of you from the youngest to the oldest. Burning Bush thank you for loving our Bishop, myself and the Shelby 5.

Finally, to everyone who I may not have listed your name that has contributed to my life (in anyway) I appreciate you. The fact that you have invested money and time to read my book speaks volumes. Thank you for your support and my prayer is that this book will be a blessing to everyone that will read and apply the words and strategies to your everyday life.

Blessings and I love you ALL...Happy Reading!

Lady Bonita Andrea Shelby

WHY NOT HAVE IT ALL!

INTRODUCTION

I sat in the midst of about 2,000 women who seemed desperate for change and a move of God. I looked around in awe as I saw the tears of those who anticipated spiritual breakthrough.

The need was great, but who would answer the call and minister to these women?

The apparent longing and undeniable desire lingered in the room as each woman awaited her personal encounter with God.

Point

God is *great* enough and *big* enough to have a "one-on-one" with everyone at the *same* time.

The anticipation in the atmosphere strengthened my desire to reach out and connect with as many women as possible in my row. I didn't speak great words of encouragement, nor did I recite a scripture, nor was my approach one of prolific or profound speech, but I grabbed as many women (by the hand) within my reach and whispered genuinely, "God loves you and you are going to make it. You are free."

These simple words (which I knew were confirmation of what they probably had heard before) brought them a release of immediate consolation and freedom. Those women, whom I personally touched, received hope and a sense of fulfillment.

Life has defining moments where we recognize that our purpose and God-ordained destiny is to care about other people. Our ministry to others should reach beyond title, the pulpit, our workplace, home and our family. You have been called to share and demonstrate the love of God to ALL people, regardless of age, race, gender, or culture. This love extends beyond religious belief and upholds the great commission...which is to extend love and the gift of salvation by example. We are *representatives* and *ambassadors* of the love of Jesus here on earth. In order to be effective we must love as Christ loves us.... unconditionally.

1 YOU DESERVE IT ALL

Everyone has the ability and power to influence others in a positive or negative way. What type of influencer are you?

As you read this book, no matter where you are in life, why not fulfill your purpose by having and doing it all?

No matter what you may have gone through in life to get to this day, *Why not have it all?*

Can you obtain all of the blessings that God has prepared for you?

Do you deserve God's goodness?

The answer is, "Yes" you deserve it, and "Yes", you can have it all! With confidence and inner drive, you can accomplish great things.

The reason that you have made it through the hurt, pain, disappointment, sickness, betrayal, depression, molestation, and heartache is that you are a survivor. The pain you've survived is evidence that you are cut from *strong cloth* and a *vessel* that God will use to bring light and hope in dark situations. Praise God for the glory that is revealed in your life with each passing day.

There is a purpose and a divine plan for your life and God has made you worthy of every blessing. The wonderful things that God has planned for the future are far greater than anything you could have ever suffered in your past.

God desires to make you whole so that you can reach out and help someone else get back on track!

This is what you deserve:

- You deserve happiness

- You deserve peace

- You deserve wealth

- You deserve health

- You deserve the promotion

- You deserve a spouse who loves you

- You deserve the absolute best

You deserve it all!!

Declare in confidence that you deserve every promise, because God's intent for your life is that you prosper even as your soul prospers. God's desire is that you are healthy as well as happy, and remember it is our Father's (God's) pleasure to give "you" the desires of your heart.

Understand what I mean when I say that we "deserve" the blessings of God. It's not necessarily because we are good and have warranted or earned great blessings, but it is by the grace of God that we live and have peace of mind to enjoy them.

Point

Never allow guilt and shame to cheat you out of
your place in the kingdom of God.

Point

Never allow your past to dictate your future

You are royalty: a princess, a diva and a king's daughter, and have therefore inherited certain benefits as a joint heir to the kingdom of God.

> "And if children, then heirs; heirs of God, and joint-heirs with Christ; if so be that we suffer with him, that we may be also glorified together." (Romans 8:17 KJV)

> "But ye are a chosen generation, a royal priesthood, an holy nation, a peculiar people; that ye should shew forth the praises of him who hath called you out of darkness into his marvelous light": (1 Peter 2:9 KJV)

The love and your acceptance of Christ confirms that you are an "heir" to everything that Christ gave to make your life successful...including His life.

EXERCISE

Luke 12:32 reminds all of us that it is God's good pleasure to give you the desires of your heart.

Write here what Luke 12:32 says

_____

_____

_____

_____

_____

_____

_____

_____

_____

_____

_____

_____

_____

_____

_____

_____

_____

_____

_____

_____

_____

_____

_____

_____

_____

_____

It is God's pleasure that you live a joyous life surrounded by those whom you love and those who love you. Then for everyone that surrounds you that doesn't love or appreciate your worth, they will become key to your growth, maturity and elevation. Haters have their place in life: to sharpen and motivate you to overcome their negativity. Don't be distracted by your opposers; learn valuable lessons from them.

Point

Trouble and a certain amount of hatred (from others) is a prerequisite to go to the next level. Make a decision to move forward, become confident and embrace success.

Somewhere down the road you may have lost your desire to be happy. Make a decision to get your life back on track, and whatever it takes—even if it takes reminiscing on some of the happiest times of your life—let's go there.

Point

The joy of the Lord is your strength. No Joy, No Strength! Choose the joy that only comes from within and choose strength!

Then he said unto them, Go your way, eat the fat, and drink the sweet, and send portions unto them for whom nothing is prepared: for this day is holy unto our Lord: neither be ye sorry; for the joy of the Lord is your strength. (Nehemiah 8:10)

Search for the happy things in life and envision the potential outcome of any situation being in your favor. You have a big God that is in control of Everything!

WHERE ARE YOU?

Along the journey called "life" you will experience many twists and turns. Your upbringing and background is key to the way you think, act and respond to situations and problems. The way in which you deal with the pressures of life is attributed to the way you perceive your life. If you have a negative view of life, then your view will be pessimistic. If you view life from a positive viewpoint, then your attitude will be positive. Your thoughts and attitude have been shaped and molded by your personal experiences, so change your mindset and way of thinking, and it will change your life. Choose to see life through a **positive** lens.

- You may have been raised in a family where there was no love shown; no hugs, no outward show of affection . . . and you were expected to know that you were loved regardless.

- You may have experienced rejection and been raised in a family where there was a difference made between you and your siblings. Perhaps you were labeled the "oddball" or the "ugly duckling."

- You may have been raised in a loving home, but somehow found yourself in a relationship darkened by domestic violence and abuse. The relationship has shattered your self-esteem and changed your positive outlook on life.

- You may be divorced, faced with starting over again with a broken heart and broken pieces.

- Are you a single parent trying to find strength and a strategy to child-rearing?

- You may feel isolated and alone due to the loss of a loved one.

- You may be faced with a terminal illness and the prognosis is not favorable.

- You may have loved ones that are sick and totally dependent on your help, resources and guidance.

- You may have aging parents and you realize that roles are slowly but surely reversing with each day.

- Someone in your family may have a mental illness and you feel helpless and drained.

- Financially, you may be struggling from week to week to pay the bills, and although you may have a great paying job, you're finding it difficult to make ends meet.

- You may have been employed at a major corporation and given your all, only to be dismissed for the wrong reasons. You may be innocent in the situation but unable to prove it.

- Your life may be one influenced by sexual perversion and promiscuity, in which everyone has labeled you.

- You may wake up every day depressed and sad because you indeed did wake up.

> **Point**
>
> Remember this: every day that you wake up, God's plan and purpose for your life is very much a reality, no matter what you may have faced the previous day.

You may be a college student failing and away from home, and you don't know how to get the help that you need to get back on the right track.

- You may be pregnant, and the thought of being a single mom is frightening because you don't feel you can take care of yourself.

- Your entire family may be jealous of your success, leaving your family relationships strained and feeling like everyone is walking on eggshells, ticking time bombs that may explode at any given moment.

- You may be in a place of depression and low self-esteem where it seems that everyone is against you.

Whatever your situation may be, I'm here to let you know that there is a way to escape. I want you to wake up, arise from the ashes and declare, "I want it all", and refuse to take down... when you can takeover! Christ died so that you might have access to greatness and He came to give you an opportunity to have it all! Take control and take it ALL back.

You can have it all because you deserve it all—whatever your ALL may be! *Why Not Have It All!*

HIDDEN TREASURES

You will never take possession of all that God has for you until you become confident in him and realize that there are hidden treasures here on Earth. Make a choice and tap into the treasure that is hidden. This *hidden treasure* encompasses all of the promises that God has declared due in your life. Each day you are in pursuit of treasure map to victory.

It is imperative that you tap into the treasure within you first, and then share (with others) your strategy of living a victorious life filled with hope.

You are treasured... a precious jewel, and don't allow anyone to make you feel otherwise. Find yourself—dig deep into your heart/soul and look for the successful and confident you!

There is someone waiting that can only be influenced by you and there are people that God has assigned to your life that can only be touched by you. It may be a smile, an encouraging word, some advice, a prayer, or a simple hug that will turn someone's life around. I encourage you to check your "sphere of influence" and use that "sphere" to connect with and help others.

Oftentimes as women we feel that in order to thrive and be happy we must live a life of isolation. We feel that the further away we stay from people, the less likely it will be that we suffer persecution or rejection. I believe that it is true that you can't allow just anyone into your circle, but I also believe that we have an obligation to treat others with respect and see the best in everyone. I also believe that Christ loves us so much, that He desires to help all of us succeed. Open up and understand that everyone isn't out to get you, and there are more that love you than you think. In order to fulfill your purpose in life and influence others, you must open up and be free.

We can't allow ourselves to become loners and secluded from society. When we wake up and realize that we exist for one another and that no man or woman is on an island, we will begin to see change in this world. It was not God's intent that you live life as a hermit locked in a cave. Realize that you need someone and someone needs you. There are honest people out there, you just need to open up and find them, and allow them to find you.

Point

When we fulfill "the great commission" which is to love others
as Christ has loved us...people become our main priority.

Know that you are a *hidden treasure*, and in order to be treasured, you must first *treasure* yourself. Know your self-worth and become a whole person. Then as you begin to *treasure* your self-worth, you will in turn treasure your gifts within and value others. As you see potential in others, you will in turn value what really matters. The "main thing" is the fulfillment of your purpose and your ability to help others find theirs.

EXERCISE
THE TREASURE LIST

Reminisce. Look back on everything that we have discussed so far. Then write a treasure list. List those things that you have locked up inside and are ready to free yourself from. Write the qualities that God has invested in your life and what you can do to change others and the world.

Finally, list your worst fears, as well as the things that you will seek courage to fulfill.

_____

_____

_____

_____

_____

_____

_____

_____

_____

_____

_____

_____

_____

_____

_____

_____

_____

_____

_____

From this day forward we will plan, strategize, and embark upon an expedition to find the real and best you and build your self-worth.

THIS IS FOR ALL OF THE MOMMIES

As a mother of five, I have lived most of my life taking care of my children who are now grown. It is definitely a transitionary period in my life. Somewhere in the shuffle of life, I took care of everyone else and placed everything in my personal life on hold. Things were stagnant by my perception, as I have always looked at life as a constant opportunity to learn how to be better and do better.

Although I was ministering to people every day, "Bonita Andrea" got lost in the shuffle. For twenty-eight years I have kept a wonderful journal of God's promises and my plan. Over the past twelve years I have gotten so busy with life, church and the wellbeing of others, that I lost the strength and desire to keep plugging at my plan.

I became too busy for strategies and planning my own life. It was about everyone else. My disclaimer is this: I never stopped caring about my appearance and fulfilling my day-to-day schedule while keeping future dreams and desires in the back of mind. But I kept everything tucked away, never taking the time needed to act on (or pull forward) future dreams. They seemed so far away and I had to trust that one day I would click back into "Bonita mode."

Then I looked up one day and "Ka-Pow!"—everyone was grown up and the time to execute came "oh" so fast. I'm thankful that I caught the opportunity, clicked into drive, pulled all the pieces together and started implementing everything in sight!

As a mother (with a growing family), your commitment to your children and family is a priority. When children mature, and the running around after them stops, you realize that your they are no longer dependent on you for everything, and you wonder . . .

"Now what am I supposed to do?"

MY STORY,
PART ONE

Today, I am navigating my way back to the fulfillment of my personal dreams and desires. Mine and my husband's primary focus, when our children were young, was to raise well-rounded children and give them a strong moral foundation.

At this stage in my life, I am now committed to not only taking care of my husband and my adult children, but to taking care of myself as well. I have found a new liberty that comes with no more bottles, diaper changes and driving my children everywhere or running a taxi service. Now when my children and I go places, I either jump in their car or hand them the keys, screaming "FREEDOM!!"

Don't get me wrong, I will never stop being a loving devoted wife, a nurturer to my children, nor a spiritual mother to the congregation. But now I realize (along with so many others) that at this stage, I have to live my life, pursue my dreams and be happy as well. I realize that I am no good to others if I am unfulfilled in my personal goals or not in direct pursuit of my destiny.

BALANCE

Here is the introduction of a word that I want you to keep in your heart and mind: Balance.

Without balance everything in your life at every stage will be out of sync.

It is time to make a commitment to balance everything in your life and give yourself time (at any given stage of life) to get back *in sync* and *on track*.

Snap your fingers, kick up your heels and celebrate today because everything past is history! Your life is on schedule and you are embarking upon a great journey.

What will you do (right now) to change your life for the better?

What can you implement to make sure that history does not repeat itself?

When balance comes "into play", your purpose will line up with your destiny, and everything will come into perspective. Balance affords you the opportunity to prioritize and operate in excellence.

Point

In every generation, and every day, we should grow wiser and stronger.
Love and appreciate your life today and *look* and *work* towards your future.
Today is here, while yesterday is gone and tomorrow is not promised.

EXERCISE
MY NAVIGATION PLAN
(WAYS THAT I CAN GET BACK ON TRACK)

Make a list of things that you can improve in your life. Then below each improvement, list the necessary steps that you must take to make them happen, e.g.:

Then map out a strategy that will help you to navigate each day and commit to finding your purpose in life.

_____
_____
_____
_____
_____
_____
_____
_____
_____
_____
_____
_____
_____
_____
_____
_____
_____
_____
_____
_____
_____
_____

Improvement #1

Step 1

_____

Step 2

_____

Step 3

_____

Step 4

_____

Step 5

_____

Improvement #2

Step 1

_____

Step 2

_____

Step 3

_____

Step 4

_____

Step 5

_____

Start with two improvements and go from there.

2 DON'T GET CAUGHT UP IN WHAT YOU ACHIEVE

According to scripture, God has given us the ability to obtain wealth, and it is God's desire that we prosper and enjoy phenomenal blessings. No matter what we accomplish, we should never forget about the *giver of life*, where we have come from and what it's taken to get there. We are blessed because of God's unmerited favor and grace. And it is by His grace that we enjoy the abundance of everything that we possess.

Society has a way of painting a picture that informs us that the only way that we are empowered or important is through popularity, influence and money. Money, popularity and influence are not the only means of empowerment. With confidence, balance and self-worth, you have every tool necessary to live a successful life.

It takes the pressure off to know that God is not biased when it comes to giving all of us the equal opportunity to live our dreams. The unmerited love that God shares speaks volumes to His desire to see everyone prosper spiritually as well as physically. God's will is that everyone prospers.

HAVE STUFF, DON'T LET STUFF HAVE YOU

> "Take heed, and beware of covetousness: for a man's life consisteth not in the abundance of the things which he possesseth". (Luke 12:15 KJV)

This scripture tells us that life is not a summation of the amount of things that we acquire or possess, but about being happy and content with what you have. Never base your self-worth on the clothes that you wear, title/position or the amount of money that you have in the bank. These things are temporal.

Recently, I had a conversation with one of my dear friends and we spoke about life and how it has to be about more than money, popularity and influence.

We strive every day to make more money and gain greater popularity, but when you check out of this life, guess what? You won't be able to take any of your material possessions with you, and with time your memory will wane and people will move on.

No matter how popular you are and how much stuff you have, it will never take the place of *true* happiness and freedom. My husband once said, "You may buy a great mattress, but you can't buy rest. You can have all the money in the world, but if you get sick, your money can't buy health." That is why it is important to be happy with life itself and realize what *true wealth* is and where it comes from: God.

Each morning that you wake up you are afforded the opportunity to fulfill your destiny. God has given you a mind to think and the ability to walk and speak. With the precious gift of life, you are in a wealthy place each day that you wake up and see your family happy, whole and healthy. That's priceless!

Realize that your purpose is not to gain popularity, money or influence, but your purpose is to carry out God's plan for your life (here on earth).

What is your plan?

What will you implement in your daily life to get you closer to your destiny?

Again, I encourage you to develop a weekly strategy. This will play a major part in the fulfillment of your purpose because you will have a template to follow. Develop a plan and commit to executing it, and each day, plug in the missing pieces and move towards the activation of your great plan. If you make mistakes along the way, grow from your mistakes and move forward.

Human nature seems to sum up a person's worth by material possessions, academic success and professional accomplishments. It is disheartening, but it is the reality of human nature.

God is just the opposite. God loves you regardless of your social status, education or reputation in the eyes of other people.

I have personally experienced situations where an individual was dressed to "the nine" and they were escorted to the front because they were viewed as affluent. On the flip side, I have witnessed those who were dressed "not so nice", and they were immediately seated in the back. People may judge on the outside, based on their perception, but God looks on the heart. God loves everyone and measures success by the fulfillment of our personal plan.

It is important to surround yourself with people who genuinely love you. I don't know about you, but I would rather be surrounded by people who love me because of my character and personality, than those who care about the amount of money, prestige or power they think I may have. I appreciate a few genuine friends more than being surrounded by fake friends.

THE PRODIGAL

The prodigal son's friends (Luke 15:11-32 KJV) were there as long as he had money and influence. I believe that it was the jealousy of false friends that encouraged the prodigal son to go to his father and pressure him into asking for all of his material things. I believe the prodigal son's friends convinced him of how protective his father was, and that he should uproot himself and discover the real world. I also believe they convinced him that he was being deprived of living his own life. This is the mentality of modern day society towards a close knit family or a relationship between parents and their children. Society feels it is abnormal for parents to love and guide their children in truth. Television, and social media influences children to break away from their parents at an early age. Family values have been compromised for so long that relationships amongst the mother and father, the children and siblings has been strained. It is almost as if children now are on a mission to prove that they are NOT close to their parents. It is satans desire to destroy "family", which is the foundational core of everything in the world.

Point

Be careful of friends who are jealous of your success and your relationship with your family (and those who love you), and in turn pressure you into leaving home. It is their dysfunction and their tumultuous relationships with their own families that seek to persuade you that what you have is dysfunctional. In fact, it's totally opposite.

The prodigal's friends lured him away from his home and hung around ~~delete him~~ as long as he had money and influence. When the money ran out, and his influence waned, they ran too. Don't be fooled or "hoodwinked" by those who really want to see your demise and in turn cause you to leave your loved ones so that (in the end) they can laugh and make a mockery of you. Make sure that you only follow the advice of those who give *sound* advice that they themselves would follow.

Satan will lure you away only to make a mockery of you in the end. This type of friend sounds just like Satan, don't they? Don't be fooled by satanic plans and plots.

The prodigal son eventually came to himself when he lost everything and said, "Why am I out here, when I have a father that loves me? The prodigal son thought about his father's servants, and the fact that they were living better than he was. I believe he became tired and headed home and realized that it was because of haters that he left in the first place.

When the father saw his son from a distance he responded as a loving father. The father ran to his son and welcomed him back home. The father was glad to see that his son was safe and the world hadn't destroyed him. The prodigal was humbled by his experience and didn't expect much but to start back to work. The father threw him a party, killed a fatted calf and put the son on a robe and gave him a ring. What a welcome reception! His brother who should have been equally happy, was a little disgruntled.

I added this

The salesperson, stunned, acted as if they had no clue what I was talking about but apologized anyway.

I continued to express my true feelings: "It's shameful how you looked on our outward appearance and sized up our worth yesterday," I said emphatically. "You didn't know who we were but you judged us by what you thought you saw—people that couldn't afford to come into your so-called "sophisticated" store."

That day was a defining moment for me that demonstrated how people are often more concerned with how you look on the outside than what is in your heart. A person may be dressed up on the outside and torn up inside. We should never limit ourselves by looking down on anyone. All people matter in the sight of God and everyone is a potential success story.

Here are some scriptures concerning the perception of wealth and material things. Read, meditate and apply them to your own experiences.

"But the LORD said unto Samuel, Look not on his countenance, or on the height of his stature; because I have refused him: for the LORD seeth not as man seeth; for man looketh on the outward appearance, but the LORD looketh on the heart".

(1 Samuel 16:7 KJV)

(19 "Lay not up for yourselves treasures upon earth, where moth and rust doth corrupt, and where thieves break through and steal:

20 "But lay up for yourselves treasures in heaven, where neither moth nor rust doth corrupt, and where thieves do not break through nor steal:

21 "For where your treasure is, there will your heart be also". (Matthew 6:19-21 KJV)

Where is your treasure?

"And he said unto them, Take heed, and beware of covetousness: for a man's life consisteth not in the abundance of the things which he possesseth". (Luke 12:15 KJV)

"For what is a man profited, if he shall gain the whole world, and lose his own soul? or what shall a man give in exchange for his soul?" (Matthew 16:26 KJV)

"For the love of money is the root of all evil: which while some coveted after, they have erred from the faith, and pierced themselves through with many sorrows". (I Timothy 6:10 KJV)

"But seek ye first the kingdom of God, and his righteousness; and all these things shall be added unto you". (Matthew 6:33 KJV)

Seek the Kingdom of God first. Kingdom principle is this; righteousness, peace and joy. Live life by kingdom principle and you will never be without blessings.... both naturally and spiritually.

I am humbled by everything that God has given my family. We may not have everything that we want, but we have everything that we need, and we are thankful.

All of the wealth that you have is on loan from God, so stay humble. God wants to trust you with so much more, and there are great blessings if you do. You may not have a whole lot of material wealth, but you have God and therefore, you have everything you need.

DON'T BECOME AN EDUCATED FOOL

It is important that we value education. Times have changed and I absolutely believe that education is crucial for this generation and the generations to come. Whatever your skill set or goals, they should always include study. The key to academic success is that you strive for excellence and make intelligent choices. It is important to embrace your ability to watch, learn and be mentored.

It is applied knowledge that will yield the making of great decisions and give you the "edge."

Parents, talk with your children about the importance of education and encourage discipline and great study habits at an early age. Start reading to your children and invest in educational tools that will promote learning. Communicate and engage in meaningful conversation with your family and realize, present day and in the future, that most jobs will require a high school education or college degree. My husband and I stress to our children and congregation that it is imperative that they pursue their education. I encourage you to do the same.

Knowledge is power on all fronts. Continue to strive to learn new things and never be complacent and think that you know everything.

Point

Education does not make you better than anyone else; there are
people who have no education that are very successful.

My father is a great example of success without a formal college education. At the age of sixteen my dad migrated to Michigan from Alabama where he married my mom and landed a job in the automobile industry. With a sixth-grade education, he worked hard and was promoted to a top management position within his corporation. He worked forty-two years as a "stellar" employee with an excellent attendance record and continued promotion. In addition, my dad was also a successful business owner and worked his nine to five job every day while running his business in the evenings.

My dad quickly rose to the top, but it was not without sacrifice. His willingness to learn and educate himself on the job and develop an excellent work history yielded him great success. My dad's determination allowed him to surpass the poverty mindset that so many have concerning their upbringing or circumstances.

My father always told me that he made it through tough times by working untiringly to make a better life for his family. My father also shared that at the age of thirteen, he began to work to help his mother and father in the home. His desire for my siblings (his children) was that we would do and be better in life than he was. I'm thankful that I married a man (my hubby) who has the same desire for our children.

When pursuing your education (on all levels) never forget about God's goodness and apply your knowledge not only in the workplace, but to advancing the Kingdom of God. Intelligence and promotion are given to you as a gift from God, and He shares those gifts so that you can in turn share them with someone else. Never feel like it is your education or intelligence that has guaranteed your success. It is only by the grace of God that you are able to learn, think and achieve.

Think about it: many people have gone to college and have degrees but have no job.

What is the deciding factor when two individuals apply for a position and one gets the job and the other is rejected? Both may have the same degree, the same level of experience, and have submitted their application at the exact same time. But only one applicant is granted the opportunity. The grace and favor of God is the deciding factor to success or failure. Therefore, it is critical that you reverence God.

It takes faith, hope and trust to receive the blessings that God has for you. Remember, without God you can do nothing.

When talking to business professionals who have climbed the corporate ladder of success, I often find they admit that with every promotion, they feel as if they move further away from their commitment to and belief in God. They became so entrenched in their career that they begin to feel as if the "God thing" is beneath them.

With corporate success, many begin to frown upon those who attend church regularly. They begin to think that it is unintelligent, even ignorant, to clap hands, jump, shout, and unashamedly declare belief in God.

If they do happen to come to a church service they sit (disconnected), holding their hands, mouths shut, and act as if praising God is reserved for the ignorant and unlearned. There is nothing further from the truth.

Remember that the more educated you are, the more knowledge and power you will add to the kingdom of God. The more money you have, the more your mentality should be concerned with giving back to those who are less fortunate. Empathize on how it may feel to live in poverty and in want of breakthrough in your life. God gives testimonies in life to prove that He is in control, and if He did it for one person, He is all-powerful and can do it again.

Point

God loves everyone

Then Peter opened his mouth and said, Of a truth I perceive that God is not a respecter of persons. (Acts 10:34 KJV)

God's love is unconditional and unbiased and He loves you whether you are good or bad. His hope is that you will wake up and become committed to fulfilling your purpose here on earth. When you reach a level of maturity that counts, with each day there lies another opportunity for you to witness the fulfillment of your goals and dreams. I believe that there should be a higher level of commitment when you receive the blessings of God. You should intensify your worship.

Point

Consider what it took to obtain the blessing; it will
take that and much more to maintain it.

And said, Naked came I out of my mother's womb, and naked shall I return thither: the LORD gave, and the LORD hath taken away; blessed be the name of the LORD. (Job 1:21 KJV)

This scripture sums up the realistic perception of one who trusts and believes that all blessings come from God.

Think about it: if God didn't wake you up and give you the mental capacity to think intelligently, or grant your health and strength, you wouldn't be able to get up, think or work.

Refuse to allow your education to make you ignorant to God's will in your life. Don't become an educated fool!

3 WRITE A VISION, MAKE IT PLAIN

"For I know the thoughts that I think toward you, saith the LORD, thoughts of peace, and not of evil, to give you an expected end." (Jeremiah 29:11KJV)

We all have dreams and things we want to do. But how do we make our dreams become reality?

My desire is that you pursue your dreams, reach your destiny and live the kind of life that God desires. If you want to attain your goals, it is important to develop a plan or roadmap. A plan of action will not only keep you on the right track, but will serve as a guide to keep you focused.

I want to encourage you . . . your dreams are very much alive. God has a specific plan for your life and the fact that you were given a dream or vision proves you can accomplish it. One thing that I have learned through my husband's sermons is that God is not playing mind games with us. When God shares his heart with you by way of a dream, a vision or insight, it is by discernment and obedience to God's will that you can align your will and actions with those God-given desires. The fact that God took time to share a dream with you is an indication that He has given you every tool to make your dream a reality.

GOD HAS A WORD OUT ON YOU

> So shall my word be that goeth forth out of my mouth: it shall not return unto me void, but it shall accomplish that which I please, and it shall prosper in the thing whereto I sent it. (Isaiah 55:11 KJV)

Everything that God has declared over your life is real and the word is activated on the earth. Although the word has been established, we must do our part. God is making good on the promise, but now we have to make good on our faith and obedience. Our only hindrance is ourselves. The word that God has declared over your life aligns with your purpose and will assist you to accomplish that which God has sent. It can't come back until it is finished. Embrace and follow the process.

LIFE HAPPENS

Life happens. At times, it seems that no one knows all that we go through (or have gone through) in our lives. We balance careers, families, and LIFE in general. To top it all off, you must deal with you!

Your mind, your will and your emotions can keep you on the infamous roller coaster of life, and your major challenge will be to win on the battlefield of your mind. Make a choice to conquer and control your thoughts.

Keep this scripture close:

> Finally, brethren, whatsoever things are true, whatsoever things are honest, whatsoever things are just, whatsoever things are pure, whatsoever things are lovely, whatsoever things are of good report; if there be any virtue, and if there be any praise, think on these things. (Philippians 4:8 KJV)

Point

Your mindset is key in achieving your goals. Think on the goods and have a positive outlook on life.

With God all things are possible, and I have learned not only to pray when times get tough, but to pray with more intensity when things are going well. Don't fall off when things are firing on all cylinders, but continue to pray. "PUSH" forward in prayer. Pray and don't stop.

No matter what happens, keep the communication lines open with God and PRAY! Keep your dream and faith alive by trusting God and realize that there is a plan and purpose for your life. God is committed to His Word.

Recognize that life is what *you* make it. As you stay with God, trust and believe in the process. Those who trust God go through trials differently than those who have no hope. We have hope because our total dependency is on God. God trusts you so much that He is giving you lots of experience to help build your résumé.

Let's look at the life of Job.

Job endured a lot of hardship in his life but he continued to trust in God to the extent that he believed everything would work out in the end. He trusted God so much that even in his trials and suffering, he took time to pray for his friend. The unselfish prayer that Job made was so monumental that it turned his captivity around. What a prayer!

Through every test we gain strength, knowledge and wisdom. Celebrate that with every test and trial, you are growing stronger every day.

When we deal with the pressures and conflicts of life, it may seem that your dreams will never come true. The enemy knows that with each passing moment you are edging closer to your victory and finish line. Oftentimes, the closer you get to your breakthrough, the greater your trials may become. It is important in trying times to stay focused on the prize and the victory. If God says it, it will happen. You are close, don't give up stay in pursuit of your breakthrough.

How can you get back on track when a trial has knocked you off course?

Here are some steps to help you make a plan and get going. This process is not as difficult as you might think, but it isn't easy either. You can use this roadmap to get started with your plan. God gives you the dream so that He can give you a plan and provisions to make it happen. If you trust God and believe, it will come true.

EXERCISE
HOW TO GET STARTED (YOUR DREAM LIST)

MY DREAM/VISION LIST

Write down your dreams and aspirations here: Write everything that you desire to accomplish in life and the expected outcome

_____

_____

_____

_____

_____

_____

_____

_____

_____

_____

_____

_____

_____

_____

_____

_____

_____

_____

_____

_____

_____

_____

_____

_____

_____

_____

_____

And the LORD answered me, and said, Write the vision, and make it plain upon tables, that he may run that readeth it. (Habakkuk 2:2 KJV)

Keep your dream list close and know that God has already made provision to make your dream a reality.

MY STORY, PART TWO

I diligently write down my dreams and what God is saying to me about my life. I totally believe in this method and even though God knows everything that we need before we ask, this tool encourages transparency in your desire to reach your personal destiny.

I have experienced success because I follow the plan of God. This doesn't mean that everything I've done has worked out, but it does mean that when there are mistakes or setbacks, I know God is going to turn my set-backs into set-ups to a victorious life.

In other words, with God in your life, success is inevitable. Everything, ultimately, will work for your good.

God makes a promise

> And we know that all things work together for good to them that love God, to them who are the called according to his purpose. (Romans 8:28 KJV)

THE SET TIME

> vs.1 To everything there is a season, and a time to every purpose under the heaven:
>
> vs.2 A time to be born, and a time to die; a time to plant, and a time to pluck up that which is planted;
>
> Vs.3 A time to kill, and a time to heal; a time to break down, and a time to build
>
> Vs.4 A time to weep, and a time to laugh; a time to mourn, and a time to dance;
>
> Vs.5 A time to cast away stones, and a time to gather stones together; a time to embrace, and a time to refrain from embracing;
>
> Vs.6 A time to get, and a time to lose; a time to keep, and a time to cast away;
>
> Vs.7 A time to rend, and a time to sew; a time to keep silence, and a time to speak;
>
> Vs.8 A time to love, and a time to hate; a time of war, and a time of peace. (Ecclesiastes 3:1-8 KJV)

Try to understand the timing and seasons of God. God's time is not our time. You can be comforted by the fact that because of our human nature, our sight is limited. Our Father (God) has foresight and hindsight; He knows our past, present and future. Trust God and know that with faith everything will happen and in fact has already happened in God's time. Walk it down and remain prayerful and focused.

Sometimes, we try hard to make things happen through our own will and power, when it is not meant to be. Or we try to force something to happen, regardless of the consequences, even at the cost of our family, spouse, and loved ones.

Always lean on God as you set goals and trust Him to attain your goals in His time.

When we move in God's timing the following is inevitable:

- When something happens, it's the right time.
- God shapes and molds us in His will as we mature.
- You learn to appreciate the downtime and you won't take things and life for granted.

- Waiting on the answer or breakthrough teaches patience.

- When you arrive and find yourself walking in your destiny you will be prepared.

- When your God-ordained opportunity/purpose meets preparation, extraordinary and supernatural things will happen.

- God will let you know that the time is right and you will know His voice.

- You will know and believe that ALL things have worked and they are working for your good.

PATIENCE IS A VIRTUE

2 My brethren, count it all joy when ye fall into divers temptations;

3 Knowing this, that the trying of your faith worketh patience.

4 But let patience have her perfect work, that ye may be perfect and entire, wanting nothing.

5 If any of you lack wisdom, let him ask of God, that giveth to all men liberally, and upbraideth not; and it shall be given him.

6 But let him ask in faith, nothing wavering. For he that wavereth is like a wave of the sea driven with the wind and tossed.

7 For let not that man think that he shall receive any thing of the Lord.(James 1:2-7 KJV)

Patience must have its perfect work in our lives. Yes, patience is a virtue and you must believe that you are destined for greatness. Wait on the Lord and be of good courage and trust God's plan against all odds and trust the process. Know that where God guides, provision has been made and the way has already been prepared for you. God's good pleasure is to give you the desires of your heart, according to His will and plan for your life. God's timing is perfect!

4 I KNOW WHO I AM, AND THAT'S OKAY

There is an ongoing identity crisis in the world in which we live. This epidemic is spreading each day in men, women and youth who strive to satisfy the world's expectations. We constantly reach toward a misconstrued view of God and a warped world standard that means that in the scheme of things we lose our "true identity."

When we conform, we transform and participate in unnatural behavior that goes totally against God's divine purpose and plan for our lives. Pure misery follows, because we exert all of our energy trying to prove to people who we are. The result of trying to please other people will often lead to a false perception of "self" and consequently an identity crisis. This ultimately leads to dissatisfaction, depression and low self-esteem.

> "I'd rather be hated for who I am and whose I am, than be loved for who I am not…. I am unapologetically me!" (Pastor Don William Shelby, Jr.)

GOD CALLS ME FRIEND

A friend is someone who is committed to your success. A true friend is compassionate, and is not jealous. They are born for hard times.

> A friend loveth at all times, and a brother is born for adversity.
> (Proverbs 17:17 KJV)

A true friend cares, is trustworthy and will tell you the truth even if it hurts. We all need friends that will stick closer than a blood brother or sister; a true friend that will stay with you in the hardest and toughest times of your life. It is a "true" friend that is solid in character, honest and committed to seeing you successful and happy.

There is a level of maturity that comes with true friendship. It also takes a certain level of maturity to desire God and place priority on your personal spiritual growth. A strong friendship is not a needy friendship, but a mutual understanding that as you grow, each person's position is to help those around them grow as well.

Point

Low maintenance relationships are those that don't require much. Mutual respect and honor remain without strain.

Point

High maintenance relationships are demanding and require constant attention.

At a very young age I made a decision that I would rather be a friend of God (who has my best interests at heart) than a "people pleaser" who denied my God-ordained destiny. Let this be the moment that you make the choice to "be" and "do" all that God has ordained you to be.

ABRAHAM -A FRIEND OF GOD

Abraham was called a "friend" of God and deemed as "The father of many nations.

Abraham left everything behind to follow the instruction of God. That speaks volumes. God's word to Abraham was to get out of his country and venture out into a land that God wanted to show him. He left the familiar and went into unchartered territory, and gave up his inheritance.

Point

There comes a time in life where you must remove yourself
from the comfortability of "the familiar", so that you can tap
into the blessings that God has on reserve for the future

With God as a friend, my enemies don't matter! Abraham knew who he was, because God told him. And the same relationship that Abraham experienced with God is available to you. I get excited every time I think about it. Abraham trusted God enough to follow the plan for his life.

We have to know who we are and whose we are and we shouldn't spend our life trying to prove ourselves or impress anyone else. If you have ever been caught up in being a "people pleaser", stop now! Don't waste your time, money or energy trying to please others. Know who you are and focus on your main objective: to develop keys to living a happy and successful life. "Do you" and be yourself!

MAIN OBJECTIVES

Here are a few components that I suggest you put into immediate action:

- Be confident.
- Strive hard to please God first—no one else takes first place.
- Remove all stress factors that are within your control to remove.
- Remove yourself from those who want you to "be" something or someone you are not.
- Surround yourself with positive role models (a mentor), friends and those who appreciate you for who you are.

- Develop friendships that help you to become a better person every day.

- Stay connected to those who can celebrate your victories and pick you up in your pitfalls.

- Develop a strong relationship with God and know His voice.

- Stay calm.

- Take one day at a time.

- Relax and stop stressing over things that are out of your control.

- Don't be distracted; remain focused and keep your eye on the prize. "I press toward the mark for the prize of the high calling of God in Christ Jesus." (Philippians 3:14 KJV)

- Set attainable goals and take the necessary steps to achieve your dreams.

- Be happy and don't worry about things that only God has the power to change.

Rest in God.

> For I know the thoughts that I think toward you, saith the LORD, thoughts of peace, and not of evil, to give you an expected end. (Jeremiah 29:11 KJV)

You have an expected end! When we recognize that God has already planned our destiny and when you take the necessary steps to reach your God-ordained purpose, you can and will not fail. There may be setbacks and detours, but failure is not an option. YOU WILL WIN!

If you haven't started your dream list yet, do it now. Your God-directed plan is a roadmap to get you from where you are to where you want to be.

5 HAPPY AND CONFIDENT PEOPLE

In this chapter we will explore six characteristics of happy and confident people.

HAPPY PEOPLE ARE RESILIENT

Happy and Confident people are strong and resilient. They have the ability to bounce back from negativity and create positives.

In order to do this yourself, understand that you can learn something from your enemies (even those that despise you). Take tough situations and trials and learn from them. When you have been wronged, mishandled or abused, use your hardship to make you a stronger and better person. Never remove yourself from how you felt during your trials, because you can effectively minister and tell your story to others at the appropriate time.

When you experience hurt or rejection, try hard not to fall into the same trap of hurting others. You know firsthand how it felt when you were ignored, violated or mistreated and because of God you made it through. Ask God for grace and the anointing to forgive those who have caused your pain. Remember the lasting effects that this violation has had on your life and then decide that you will not subject others to this pain (past or present). A resilient attitude and spirit will allow you to be an effective witness to the redeeming and healing power of God.

HAPPY AND CONFIDENT PEOPLE DON'T HATE, THEY CELEBRATE.

It is important that you celebrate when people are doing better than you. Don't be a hater. God does not want you to be jealous and petty.

My husband says, "You cannot extract from an anointing that you despise." Having the right attitude can be a key to your future blessings. When you appreciate the talent, gifts and the anointing of someone else, God can trust you with everything that has been placed on reserve for your life. Despising another person's anointing only sets you back.

Remember jealousy is as cruel as the grave, meaning that the grave has no mercy, no compassion, and it grips you and won't let you go. Only dead things are grave-side, and there is no life there.

The fact is, if you want more, surround yourself with those who are living your dream. Take the lid off! Many women can't stand to see their sisters prosperous and happy. Think about it and realize that jealousy will always keep you at a disadvantage. Until you learn to celebrate others, you won't experience the good life. Let's face it, there will always be someone capable, better looking, shapelier and more educated than you. Face reality. It takes nothing away from your *fabulousness* to commend someone else on their "fabulousness"! Practice and rejoice with those that rejoice! Celebrate you, celebrate life, and celebrate someone else. Take your measure, know who you are, and work at optimum level with what God has given you! After all, there is nobody on this earth like you.

My father would always say, "Don't walk around feeling like you are better than anyone else, but know this: you are just as good as anyone else."

When we begin to understand that we ALL have something to give, we will take all of our differences, opinions and life experiences and do something great for God.

HAPPY AND CONFIDENT PEOPLE GIVE BACK

Know your capabilities and if you lack in a certain area, surround yourself with people that can help you. Watch, learn and observe. That is the trait of a true Queen. God's girls give back and give to others. You are great when you help someone else achieve their goals and become great. If you have the right attitude, you can be a tool to help someone else discover their "greatness." It takes nothing away from you and actually it is a testament to how wonderful you are when you help someone else achieve their dreams. Just think about it, you may be the blessing that someone else has been praying for. So while pursuing your personal dream, help someone else along the way.

HAPPY AND CONFIDENT PEOPLE FORGIVE

I'll talk about this in upcoming chapters, but it's important to keep yourself free of resentment and unforgiveness. Some things are harder to forgive than others, but God is able to give you the grace to forgive. Just as God forgave us, try to let go and open up so that the love of God will overflow and take away all of your hurt and pain. When we forgive, we in turn take the power out of the enemies' hands. Make a choice to forgive and experience all of the freedom that happiness brings.

HAPPY AND CONFIDENT PEOPLE DESIRE TO SEE EVERYONE AS GOD SEES THEM

We are all in need of improvement. Know that everyone has a purpose and some have just failed to embrace their God-ordained plan for their life. You are the bigger person: a leader and vessel that will be used as a light on Earth to encourage others to reach their fullest potential. You cannot assist others until you confidently know who you are in God and also see the hidden inner potential of others. Understand that everyone's journey in life may look very different than yours. If you took the time to explore their lives you would find that every one of us is a victim of our circumstances, whether good or bad. We are all sinners saved by grace. Without God's grace, where would we be? Extend that grace and mercy to others and don't be critical. Remain confident that God can save everybody, including you!

HAPPY AND CONFIDENT PEOPLE KNOW THEIR SELF-WORTH

You are priceless—one of a kind. Never put yourself in a position in which you need constant validation from other people. Know your strengths and work on your weaknesses. Weakness does not mean hopelessness. We all have weaknesses. When we recognize our insufficiencies, it keeps us working on ourselves. Never reach a place of complacency; keep it real with yourself. Know your conviction in regard to God's plan for your life and stick to it. Follow the plan.

Many times I will get up to do something and with a microphone in hand, I feel a "surge of nervousness." One day while riding in my car, I asked God, "Why is it that every time I am on stage to do something, I experience fear?' "When will I get over it? I asked. God replied and said, "Never, because the moment you get over it, you will no longer be dependent on my guidance and anointing." God said, "I have to keep you with a certain level of nervousness, so that you will understand how dependent you are upon My help as you minister to My (God's) people. A bright light came on, and I realized that nervousness is my "built in" mechanism to keep me grounded, growing and dependent upon God's presence and not my own abilities. It is God that makes us great. From that day forward, whenever I am asked to speak, sing, etc.. part of my prayer time and before going on stage, I say, "Okay Lord, I'm depending on you, It's just me and you, and with you I have everything I need."

The initial feeling of being nervous is always present, but after I get "in the zone", its full speed ahead.

MY STORY,
PART THREE

I realized early in life that I was different. I had a different perspective than most people my age. I couldn't get involved in a lot of things that my classmates or others did. Many times, my peers thought I felt that I was better than everyone else and called me "Miss Goody Two-Shoes." That certainly was not the case. I just had my personal conviction and a God-directed course to follow. I never allowed situations or the opinions of others to force me to ignore my convictions. Peer pressure was never a big issue for me. I was strong-willed and although I didn't know then my exact destiny in life, I did know it was positive and that God was preparing me for something great.

I accepted Jesus as my personal savior at the age of sixteen and began to seek God's plan for *my* life. God told me to remain pure and a virgin until I was married. He also told me I was not to date anyone. No boyfriends, friends only. At the same time, God also told me I would not know a man sexually until after I married.

I will never forget, in the ninth grade, one of my few friends at high school talking about dating a boyfriend. I thought to myself, "Wow, God just gave me all of these rules and my friends are doing whatever they want. This is so unfair!"

TWO POINTS

Point #1: What's Good for Everyone Else May Not Be Good for You.

Ninth grade is typically a time when everyone begins to change emotionally and physically. My classmates and I had remained close throughout elementary and middle school. But by the beginning of ninth grade, everyone's priorities and mind-sets had changed. All of a sudden, my close-knit relationships became distant, and everyone began to move into new ways of life. They all thought they were grown up now and acted like we had never been friends.

I noticed the changes going on with my peers; some of it was good and some of it was not so good.

Parents, it is imperative that when your child starts school, you take the time to talk with them about right and wrong. Talk to them about choices and consequences. Encourage them to make quality decisions regarding what path they will take. During their teenage years, major decisions are made that will determine their life's direction and impact their character. You should always encourage your child to stay on course toward their destiny and not necessarily follow the path of a friend or the crowd.

Point #2: Recognize That Times Have Changed

Times have definitely changed since my generation was in high school, and while my parents didn't have to worry about talking to me about certain things early on, this generation moves a lot quicker toward adulthood, so we must be proactive in teaching them early on. As parents, educators and mentors, we must prepare ourselves to teach the hard subjects and talk about those things that no one wants to talk about. As we move into the future, we must approach the truth with no fear. As times change, truth must remain the same and certainly God's word never changes.

PEER PRESSURE

Peer pressure is an important topic of discussion. I have found out over the years that peer pressure is common in elementary school and certainly throughout our children's educational careers.

With social media and a constant connection to the outside world, children have to deal with a lot of distractions. Our children are connected to the "cyber world" twenty-four hours a day. Children replace family time with video games and the Internet. It is critical that parents monitor their children on the Internet, and become educated enough to keep up with who their children are connecting with and talking to. Pop-ups and subtle satanic messages are real.

When my children were young I would investigate even the cutest cartoons, and if I picked up (through my discernment) on a subtle satanic message, or if the cartoon was morally corrupt, I would not allow them to watch it. Know who and what your children are plugged into. Be aware that porn sites are easily accessible, through pop-ups and social media; a tactic of Satan to force your child to stay connected to this sinful world. Disconnect yourself and your child from anything that won't bring positive results.

THE BIG BAD BULLY

Bullies are on the rise and intimidation runs rampant in our schools, the workplace and in life. As a parent, you must realize that your child enters a war zone each day when they go to school. (Some of you enter a "bully zone", when you get to work.) For some of your children, the war zone starts on the bus or at the bus stop and not just the classroom or the playground. Make sure that home is a place of peace and acceptance. It is important that home becomes the safe haven for your child to open up a dialogue and strategize counterattacks to the plans and tactics of Satan that aim to destroy our youth. For those who enter a "bully" work zone, it is also important that you make your home, your office (cubicle), or car, your place of refuge or rest. That means, when bullied in the workplace, steal away, take a deep breath, and get back to work! I might add- pray about someone that you can confide in that will give sound advice to how to deal with the situation.

Parents, we have to give positive solutions to sometimes unpleasant circumstances. Tell your child that they don't have to fall prey to or become entrapped in the norm. Stress the importance of their relationship with God, and teach them to be strong in what they believe. All that matters at the end of the day is that we continue to grow in grace and become all that God has called us to be.

When adults deal with bullying it is imperative that they stand their ground and remain confident. At the appropriate time, let the bully know that you will not succumb to their tactics and plots to demean your character and be in control of your life.

We are never too young nor too old to become friends of God. When we accept our true identity and submit our life to God, there will be no amount of peer pressure that will be powerful enough to derail our future. Embrace God's unique identity because we are fearfully and wonderfully made, with a purpose. You are one of a kind.

MY STORY, PART FOUR LIFE ONLY GETS BETTER

Many women think that things go downhill after forty. I want to start a new trend, and a new way of thinking. On my fortieth birthday, I had an encounter with God and He spoke to me and said, "Now is the time to develop, be at peace, take the pressure off and live your best days. It's time now to live your life to 'its' fullest, because now you have gained so much experience that you have built a great resumé in God. Prepare to enter into Canaan—a land that is filled with "big"," God said, "Now get ready to live your best days."

At "fabulous" 40, I was at ease and set free from the pressure of people and life itself. My sole motivation and focus was in completing the assignment that God gave to me. I am dedicated to helping others to gain a desire to better themselves, and this book is the product of my assignment.

God went on to tell me, "Don't focus on negative people who have constantly kept their foot on your neck. Direct your energy to spending time with those who value who you are as a person. No longer spend the majority of time with those who constantly drain you and never pour back, but start to surround yourself with people who have your back, and not their back to your face."

I've learned that people can pour into each other in a variety of ways. Some pour into others by praying for them, giving them compliments, encouragement, or simply being "low maintenance" friends that bring no drama. I love relationships where I don't have to measure up: I can simply be me.

As a Pastor's wife, I am heavily involved in ministry and constantly carrying others. I am learning each day to appreciate those who require nothing more than to love and embrace my humanity. They are open to the love that I give them and they give love in return. I honor people who appreciate and at least try to understand what my husband/children and I go through on a daily basis.

We have (at some time or another) encountered those individuals that feel like they do just as much or more, and are experts on every subject. No one is an expert on everything. If someone feels unteachable, they will remain ignorant. Ignorance says, "I know it all." I have learned (the hard way), that people who don't value my advice, I simply find someone who will. At this stage of my life, everything that I do has to count. I have no time to waste.

My husband shared that it really puts a person at a disadvantage when they walk into a room of experts acting like a "know-it-all." When they open their mouth they appear unlearned and ignorant because what they fail to realize is that the individual that they are offering advice to is indeed the expert. You can never learn if you don't listen and realize that you DON'T have all of the answers. No one person knows everything, that's why we have one another.

When a Pastor and his wife are connected to the heart of the people whom they serve, no one can really understand the constant spiritual weight and warfare that those two people carry. For the individual in the pew that feels they are equally stressed . . . They are clueless.

While I am the Pastor's wife, there are times when I don't feel exactly what the Pastor feels, but I strive hard to stay compassionate and connected to what my husband may be going through. I am also considerate regarding his direction in how to deal with the people to whom we have been called to minister. Remember this, that a Shepherd's heart is different to any other heart.

It becomes aggravating when the people in the pew who attend church for a couple hours on Sunday and run out of the door until the next Sunday feel as though they can run the church more efficiently than their Pastor. It is important that congregations understand that the Pastor and his family's life is the church and its people, which is not always easy.

The lifestyle of a Pastor is not only about Sunday mornings; he is on call seven days a week, twenty-four hours a day. Unlike a doctor who can go on call, complete their shift and go home for the day, the Pastor is always on call and always in rotation. The Pastor has a pager that's always on.

My husband and I experience hectic days and at times we are up all night praying. We wake up the next morning, back to counseling sessions, hospital visits, and phone calls in the middle of the night. Life in ministry is never-ending and there is always something to keep you occupied.

I might mention the 4am call, when the person on the other line asks, "Were you asleep?" That becomes a bit frustrating. Then you find out their reason for calling is that they have a headache and can't sleep. "Well now that makes three of us, and my entire household has been disturbed". The 4 am call always breaks my rest and my heart beats fast because you always feel that something tragic has happened. Nevertheless, the person on the other end of the line feels that they are in a dire situation, so who is to judge?

When you genuinely care for people, you realize that, to them, their needs may seem like a matter of life and death. Because they are God's people and they have been entrusted into our care, we are obligated to help them feel better, no matter what the situation.

For every person who feels as if they can do a more efficient job of being in charge of the church, I encourage them to switch places with their Pastor for one day. It's easy to look on and complain and murmur from the pew. I guarantee that after twenty-four hours their opinion would be totally different, and they wouldn't be so quick to criticize.

WALK IN THESE SHOES

Nothing becomes more aggravating than a member that continues to tell people, and the Pastor's family, that they totally understand what a Pastor's family endures, while they continue to disregard and dishonor their Pastor and his family. This is unacceptable, and I believe that when you have a Shepherd that genuinely loves his people and is committed to the wellbeing of his congregation, he—or she—is worthy of respect and honor. When an individual disrespects leadership, there is always a consequence. I believe in the biblical principle of the *sower* and *reaper*—in other words, "you reap what you sow".

Unless you walk in these shoes, you will never know the sacrifices that a pastor's family makes to care for the souls of the people whom they serve.

Let's be clear, there are members who feel the heart of their leader, and I salute those who continue to pray for and support their leader with a pure and honest heart. I encourage those who gossip and are on a satanic mission to make life hard for their man and woman of God (and their family) to stop, and have a heart for the one who has been placed to watch over your soul.

As a Pastor's wife, I believe in the great reward and inward peace that comes from serving the people of God. Above everything, it is an honor and a privilege that my husband was called by God to help guide and direct people by example, preaching a life changing Word and giving their lives as a "living sacrifice ". There is a sense of fulfillment when you see lives transformed and mindsets changed before your eyes. Ministry to God's people is rewarding as well as challenging. We have accepted the challenge.

MINISTRY BALANCE

Eve was Adam's "help mate". In my opinion a help mate is a balancer. Eve was the nurturer, mother and wife all in one. She helped to bring balance to her husband and her children.

It takes balance to be effective in life and ministry. The role of a Pastor or Pastor's wife has to include balance and commitment to the "big picture."

ARE YOU PURPOSE DRIVEN OR GOAL DRIVEN?

We should be "purpose driven" instead of "goal driven". Look at it from this perspective: your goals are to get from A to B, but your purpose is from A to Z. Your purpose (A to Z) is what you have been put on this planet for and your destiny-driven goals (A to B) help you walk in your purpose.... step by step.

You may have mega goals and only have fulfilled three of them. Does that make you a failure? The answer is "no", because your purpose is being fulfilled every day. Your purpose may be praying for the sick, ministering to the hurt, or meeting the needs of your family. All of these things are happening in the midst of you meeting your personal goals and walking in your purpose.

We should never access our self-worth solely through attaining our biggest goals, but be confident in our purpose every day. If you are an individual that is strictly goal-oriented, you won't feel successful in life or ministry, because the need is never-ending.

Effective ministry is this: as soon as you complete one assignment, the next one starts. You must carry a sense of accomplishment in that your assignment is people, and people change and the need remains.

You must also be self-motivated and encourage yourself, and do your best. Never base your worth on the accolades of others, because oftentimes people feel that most men and women in ministry don't need encouragement because they are strong and resilient. I beg to differ; they need much encouragement, because guess what? They are human too.

Take the time to encourage your Pastor or leader. Let them know that you respect and honor the words of life that come forth every Sunday, Tuesday or whatever your day of worship. Take time to let their spouse know that you love them and appreciate the sacrifices that they make every day, and lastly pull the children together and let them know that you love them and that you sincerely want God's best for them. Think about it: The Pastor continually carries the congregation in their heart and prayers, but who will have a heart and carry the Pastor and his family? If you love your Pastor, you will love what they love.

As the Pastor balances ministry and life, you must do the same in whatever position or place that you hold in ministry.

Remember that when you balance ministry and life it is important that you also encourage yourself. Know God's plan and purpose for your life and fulfill it.

Point

Don't be guilty of the church member that purposely "shuts down" the "first family", just because you feel as if they get too much attention. This is a satanic plot to wreak havoc on those that have been placed in leadership. Ask God to touch your heart so that you will understand that the first family(or anyone in leadership) is constantly on the firing line and it is total opposite of what people think.

Save Yourself in the Process

In ministry, it is important to face the fact that it is not humanly possible to help or save everyone. Neither will you please everyone. We are helpers of God and we will never graduate in our service to people. As soon as you feel that you have seen it all, another situation proves otherwise. God will give you a "Deal with it as it comes" grace. You will never know everything and as you learn every day, you will grow in grace, wisdom and knowledge.

Again, the role of a Pastor and Wife are never-ending. There is always something to do in the Kingdom of God. It is important that a Pastor, his wife and family surround themselves with people who genuinely love them, pray for and support them. I say "genuinely", because no one needs people who say that they love them in their presence and talk about them cruelly behind their backs. A Pastor and wife also need those who Do Not in a subtle way circumvent their authority. Example; The Pastor/give instruction or an assignment to a staff leader. In the presence of the Pastor they totally agree with what has been said. But as soon as the Pastor leaves, the "so called" leader rejects everything the Pastor says in the presence of their peers. This is not acceptable as it confuses others as to what a "real leader" is and creates hardship as it pertains to the growth of a department, etc... It then becomes hard for others to follow that leader because from that point forward trust has been broken. They move from being a trusted leader to the Pastor and wife to one that has to re-build confidence in their leadership.

It is also important to surround yourself with people who are not jealous of your success and those who are not in (constant) competition with you. It's time to do a self-check if you are bothered (and not happy) when someone else is successful. A spirit of competition will cause one to go bankrupt. Celebrate the success of others and it will pave the way for your "Big Break"

In order to walk effectively in ministry (and life), a leader must know if they can trust "in" and "outside" of their circle. Once that trust is broken, it is hard to gain it back. It's important in life to be one that is trustworthy and honest.

The Pastor's family also needs moments to shut down and regroup as a family and pour into each other. Remember, Pastors, that you were called by God, but your spouse and children were not called in the same way. I believe that God knows what is needed to complete your assignment here on Earth, especially when you marry in God's will.

If you are a Pastor's wife, lift the pressure off and keep track of your personal victories so that you can feel a sense of accomplishment.

Point

You cannot be ALL things to everyone, only God can.

Don't feel guilty about taking time out, going on family vacations where you don't answer the phone, and spending valuable time with your spouse and family. Don't beat yourself up about what you cannot humanly accomplish. I want you and your spouse to live a peaceful and long life. There may be times when peace isn't around you, and people's expectations of you are more than you can bear. In those times take a "time out", to pray and evaluate what is being required and what is actually needed. Check your heart, ensure that you have given all that's humanly possible and hold on to the peace giver and embrace inner joy. Keep a pure heart "full of love.'

OFF THE BLOCK

The older I become, the more I appreciate those who don't have me on the auction block to the highest bidder. I say "auction" block because fair weather friends will sell you out for the next popular person. I desire friendships and relationships that reflect this: As I honor their worth, they in turn honor my worth. Iron sharpens iron.

All relationships should be cordial, but when you find yourself constantly exerting all of your energy in a relationship it becomes exhausting. Make sure that your investment yields something more than heartache and a constant "tug-of-war".

Don't fight over anything that won't bring you spoils. Fight only one fight: the good fight of faith.

> Fight the good fight of faith, lay hold on eternal life, whereunto thou art also called, and hast professed a good profession before many witnesses. (1 Timothy 6:12 KJV)

People whom you have to walk on eggshells with and need to constantly reaffirm that you love, will continually drain you and give nothing back. Love them and let them go. It takes too much time and energy to continue to carry dead weight. You will find that they could walk all along, but just wanted the convenience of being carried and catered to. When you enable and empower others to stand strong on their own two feet—that is the trait of a good leader.

Our position is not to cripple or make others dependent on our abilities; the ultimate goal is to equip others to be dependent on God and themselves, and to grow to their independence so they can reach their destiny and thrive.

The fact is we must deal with all personalities whether we choose to or not. The key is to seek God's guidance in how to deal with each individual according to the way God deals with us. Learn to administer the gift of mercy and then restore each person without inflicting more pain or aggravating the wound. Keep your spirit clear and remain open and free so that the love of God can flow through your life.

A LEVEL OF MATURITY

When you reach a certain level of maturity, those opportunities to "be you" and surrounded by people who love you unconditionally, matter the most. I appreciate intimate gatherings in which everyone is pouring and there is no selfish ambition. It means more now in my life to be surrounded by a few people that genuinely know who I am than to hang with the masses of which basically half of the crowd is there to criticize, spectate or in need of attention.

I oftentimes wonder why it's the crowd that dictates a person's worth. In our world we deem our importance by the number of people that attend our churches, our birthday parties, baby showers and weddings, etc.

I had a defining moment one day as I sat in a restaurant with a few members of our staff. They had arranged my private surprise birthday lunch at a well-known restaurant. I had a wonderful lunch with women who genuinely wanted to be in my presence for no other reason than to celebrate my special day.

I looked around the room and saw another small group of ladies who were celebrating a daughter's baby shower. This was an *eye opening* experience as I witnessed a group of ten ladies come together to celebrate the birth of a baby. The group as a whole seemed so happy and the three tables were filled with gifts. There were so many gifts (sixty at least)! I thought, "Wow! There have to be more people than I see. How could just ten ladies give all of these gifts?" Note: I have attended showers with fifty to a hundred people where there were only three gifts on the table. Not only that, the food would be free and an individual would have the audacity to come to the shower, eat lots of food and not bring a gift. We all know common etiquette: you never arrive at a shower, birthday or wedding celebration empty handed. If all else fails at least pick up a card. I'll talk about this more in my next book on etiquette!

Back to my defining moment. This was the day that I realized how important it is to be surrounded not by the masses, but by people who genuinely want to see you do well and who are genuinely concerned about your happiness.

The fact is, as you age you have to grow your personal circle of friends. It is no one person's responsibility to attend your birthday celebration if they don't know you or do not have a close relationship with you. People should not expect someone to attend their event and bring a gift when they aren't friendly or never speak. That sounds absurd and makes absolutely no sense. Yet I have witnessed people get upset and throw shade on the church with claims like, "there is no love in this church, and nobody likes me." Watch those who get made, the response never fails of; "that church ","this church", and "your church ", no longer embrace their church home and take ownership. This is a characteristic of a "blame-shifter."

What they fail to realize is that the church is not responsible for cultivating personal friendships. Just like in the world, you can't force people to be friends, nor can you make anyone do *anything for* that matter. Keep in mind that you must show yourself friendly if you desire friends. It is selfish and unfair to think that people have to do anything for you, and if they do show up at your event, you should deem it a kind gesture from the heart. Remember, no one owes you anything. It is a victim's mentality that feels as if everyone owes you. A victim's mentality can also be identified as the feeling that nobody likes you, everyone is out to get you, and you are mistreated and overlooked.

Point

Increase your circle of friends, and show yourself friendly
so that when you need friends, it won't be difficult to find
those with whom you have built relationships with.

I have been in so many situations where this has been the case. Some feel that because I am the Pastor's wife I am obligated to host showers and birthday parties. If I choose to throw someone a shower or a party, it is my prerogative. Many days (sometimes against my will), I would follow my desire or husband's request and throw someone a party(shower) whom I knew didn't appreciate it, but by doing what God told me to do, I was no longer responsible at that point. Once you know your heart and what God is saying, that's enough. Do your part and then put everything else in God's hands.

As a Pastor's wife, my Hubby and I never want our congregation to feel slighted in terms of special events in our family's life. We decided that, as much as we were able, we would always let our entire congregation know of special events in our lives. That way, if they didn't show up, the ball was in their court; they could not say that they weren't invited. Of course there were situations where we could not invite everyone, and that's where it would take the maturity of the congregation to understand what was and was not humanly possible.

FIFTY AND STILL FABULOUS

Age forty: I came into Canaan—the Promised Land!

At age fifty, I had another defining moment: to embrace "Bonita" and learn my self-worth while forgetting those who didn't value me. The day I received revelation, I ran to my Hubby and shared my spiritual awakening and he in turn rejoiced and said, "Baby girl, get ready to live."

I am now confident in who I am and in my capabilities. I have confidence in whom I serve and appreciate my design.

Where for years I had begun to close myself off and put things on reserve, waiting for the right time, the Lord now told me that the time was now!! It was time to open up.

God told me that I was putting myself on reserve. You can place yourself on reserve for a certain group of people who become complacent. I noticed that the same group of people that once loved me and thought that I was the best now thought I was boring and my life was mundane. If you are the ministry's "First Lady," you can't allow people to hold you hostage. Many pastors' wives are held hostage by their attempts to please everyone to the point of being miserable. Or the Pastor's wife remains stagnant to continue to minister to the same group of people that are selfish towards the idea of their Pastors wife developing new relationships.

Point

Don't allow people to hold you hostage or tie you up with their opinion of other people. Never take another person's opinion (of someone else) for face value.

When women are at odds with someone, they often expect you to be at odds with that person as well. In such circumstances, if you are not careful, you will find yourself the ringleader of "The First Ladies Gang." No one can come in and no one can go out. My place has always been to minister to and love everyone. I offer no apologies.

I refuse to allow people to make me respond the way they want. I refuse to be the puppet on the string controlled by others' emotions. I love everyone and will always get to know people for myself. It is weakness when women listen to other people's opinions about someone before they get to know the person for themselves. Never allow members of your church or even in the workplace to dictate to you who you can talk to and who you can't. I have worked extremely hard to open my heart just as Christ has opened His heart... for all people.

If Jesus had enough love in His heart for everyone, and I'm striving every day to be like Jesus, then my heart should be big as well. I know that some people are more difficult to love than others, but we have still been commissioned to love them in the way that we are loved by God: unconditionally. I may not like what someone does or how they act towards me, but I refuse to hold on to hatred and bitterness in my heart.

DON'T CLOSE YOURSELF UP

Never close yourself up from people who want to be close. Don't fall prey to the thought, "I don't want to be in nobody's mess, so I'll stay by myself." Realize that when you open yourself up, God has your back and wants you to explore new relationships. Everyone is not messy and there are wonderful people out there who will place great value on you as a person. God has your back.

HUMBLE PIE

Humility is a wonderful attribute, but when it is taken to the extreme it can be harmful. Have you encountered individuals who say they are humble (by word), but their actions speak opposite? Or, are you like the individual that when you're given a compliment you diffuse it by saying something like, "This is so old, or "I'm trying, but feel so inadequate, etc.... When someone gives a compliment, say "thank you" and leave it at that. Don't try to downplay the compliment by saying something negative. This is something that I am continually working on in my personal Life-Just say "thank you" and carry on.

Depending on how you were raised, you may have been taught that a confident person is arrogant. What we fail to realize is this, you can be "so" humble that you operate in pride. If you are humble and you use it to seek attention and to impress people with how "humble you are", that is false humility. If you view every confident person as arrogant, you are *self-righteous*.

Point

Saying "thank you "does not make you proud. It is an acknowl-edgement of the truth or the acceptance of a kind word.

Isolation and Betrayal

Isolation primarily is a result of, hurt, betrayal and rejection. Some ladies are isolated and don't trust *anyone*. They constantly feel betrayed and rejected and live a life of watching their backs and thinking everyone is up to something. They "eye" every female because they feel that people (women in particular) try to get close in order to steal their husbands and find out their business. It is abnormal when an individual is always skeptical towards everything. It is not always the case that when someone is kind, that they are trying to get close to hurt or harm you. I admit that dealing with—and particularly leading—women is not always easy, but God will anoint you with the grace to *keep it real* and keep your heart pure.

> **Point**
>
> Ask God for discernment so that you will recognize those true God-sent relationships and not live a closed and miserable life.

There are some genuine, true people that have been sent into your life and ministry to help. There are people that have been sent into your life to help you get to the next level. Be strengthened and know that God will take care of you and everything that pertains to you. He has your best interests at heart and will protect that which concerns you and your family.

Be mature, be the bigger person, then realize that God has called you to be a light to so many others. Open up your heart to everyone and allow God to guard your heart. Don't hold back in developing new relationships for fear that people will think you are trying to be wonderful. Open up! You are Free! Free to fulfill your purpose. Free to love and be loved.

At fifty I awoke to my purpose.

ONE OF A KIND

This book is the first of many assignments that I will complete in my life. While I put many things on hold for various reasons, I absolutely have no regrets. Now God says, "Ready, set, go!" It's my time. And it's your time!

Whether you are fifty, nineteen, sixty or a hundred, you are *one of a kind*, so celebrate and be thankful each day (starting now). Embrace the divine plan God has for your life. There may be pit stops and detours along the way, but the key is to keep moving. Don't give up!

Your turnaround starts today when you recognize that your story has already been written and the outcome is happily ever after!

OWN YOUR STORY

Place value on *your* life and *your* journey. Don't discredit it. Everyone's story has meaning and can actually help someone else. Don't be ashamed. Be transparent, and share.

Your story to date is a tribute to your personal survival—your journey through life. As you embrace each day, you will gain a greater sense of appreciation for the ability to explore a brand new day. Each one presents an opportunity to fulfill your destiny. Life then becomes a daily walk, and with each step, possibilities <u>awaken.</u> It is with confidence that we recognize that happiness matters, and <u>self-worth</u> is a key component to happiness and ultimate success.

Let's go and make life happen! The time to do *you* is now! Be the best that *you* can be.

Make a decision to free yourself from the pressure of making everyone else happy. To think that everyone will be happy is a utopian fantasy. It will never happen. I can remember praying, "Lord, can you just give us one day when everyone is happy?"

THE SERVICE, PROFESSIONAL'S PLIGHT

To every professional that provides help or service or if you deal with the wellbeing of people: know that because you care for people, there will always be someone in need. For every person, there are at least three problems/issues. More people, more issues. This can (at times) become stressful and over barren when you are compassionate towards the needs of others. At times, it can be depressing when you can't help EVERYBODY, and the people that you helped most, may not appreciate your sacrifice.

In the church, my husband and I would say, "The more members we have, the more problems we will have to deal with and pray for." We were called to minister to the needs of people.

No longer blame yourself for other people's problems. You can offer solutions, but at the end of the day the individual has to put that plan in motion. I can remember times when I could see the spiritual attack on people in the church, particularly the women. The moment you rescued one from a bad attitude (or problem), another would catch "the spirit", or (bad attitude). You had no clue that they had a problem, with you to begin with. When a second person caught the same problem (the spirit), you recognize at that point it is spiritual warfare.

You love and rescue one person from going over the cliff (of a bad feeling) and that is the moment the same spirit overtakes another member and they start acting crazy and running for the cliff. It is never ending. I have learned not to lose heart because not everyone can be happy all the time. I have to love them as they are and keep my heart pure. If I try hard to keep my heart pure then God knows I am good.

When the majority of your efforts and your life is lived to convince others to appreciate their self-worth, you will become tired, frustrated and worn. Realize that the only assistance that you give only goes so far, but God can change the heart or internal. Take the pressure off and make yourself happy. Never stop loving others, and pouring into their lives. Please God and follow His plan for your life. And remember, those who discredit you or don't appreciate you . . . they lose.

6 TWO VOICES, TWO CHOICES

Life is choice driven, and your life is the summation of the choices that you've made.

Our lives are filled with decisions that can shape and move us toward our destiny, or lead us further away from our best life. Small decisions such as which dress or what shoes to wear, and major decisions such as who to marry, what job to take, or where to live. Every decision big or small have consequences, and, like it or not, where we are today being the grand total of all of those choices, big and small.

As a child, I recall watching my favorite cartoon. Each Saturday I would sit in my chair and relax with a bowl of cereal. This particular Saturday, I watched a character face a defining moment. Suddenly, out of nowhere, appeared a little character on each shoulder. One was "good" (with a halo) and the other was the "bad" (wearing red and holding a pitchfork). The good was softly spoken; the other was angry and loud. The character (with the halo), spoke with a soft voice, and would encourage peace and patience and longsuffering. In other words, it spoke goodness and encouraged the "right thing." The other spoke evil and encouraged an outrageous response. The evil voice said things such as, "Don't take that from them, beat them down!" and "Who do they think they are?"

The images in that cartoon stuck with me throughout my life, because I realized that it wasn't far from reality.

When the time comes to make a decision, there are two voices and two choices. The big question is; which voice are you going to listen to? Good or evil? Will you listen to God, or the devil?

There is always a decision to make at critical moments in our lives. When you stand at the crossroads, which way should you go? And how can you know that the decision is the right one?

The key to making good choices is living a life that is connected to the love of God. As you develop a relationship with God, the basis of your actions, as well as your responses, will be motivated by your desire to please God and love. There will be times when you feel like you have extended yourself to the maximum. There will be times when you become confused as well as exhausted from loving others and seeing others the way that God sees them. It takes work.

LOVE IS AN ACTION WORD

We must make a choice to love. Love is more of a choice than an action. You must make a choice to love others just as Christ loves you. If you are married, you must make a choice to love your spouse. The wedding vow is serious and more than catchy rhetoric. They are vows of commitment and sincerity before God. Look closely at the wedding vow that we make at the altar. Are we saying things to hurry up and get the ceremony over with? Are we caught up in a fairy tale moment? Are we not taking seriously one of the biggest decisions that we will ever make in life? Do we really understand what we are saying?

I am asked all the time, "What is the key to a good relationship?"

Although sexual intimacy is important, you have to love that person beyond sex. Love beyond physicality is a key component to what makes a long, lasting relationship.

TIME AND CHANGE

Time will always bring about familiarity, and certain events can cause you to have a different mentality when it comes to love. If love in marriage is based on emotion alone, then we are all doomed and headed for divorce court or separation! If true love is to last, it has to be something deeper: a choice and a will to love unconditionally, the same way that God loves us.

Can someone really maintain the same feeling of love and commitment for forty, fifty, sixty years? The answer is "yes".

We all know that over time, the physical body ages and change is inevitable. Hair starts to gray or fall out, tight supple young skin sags and eyes grow deep and dim. Everything that was once young, tight, vibrant and new becomes *old* and *slow*.

Relationships based on physical attraction and sexual feelings alone won't last. As time goes by, you and your spouse will grow older. He may lose the six pack and you may lose that hourglass figure, and then what?

Over time, every relationship must develop into something more than physical. True love is not based solely on physical appearance. Initially it is physical appearance that attracts the opposite sex. You see first, then explore. Then, it comes down to your decision to love no matter what your spouse looks like. Key factors come into play: maturity, commitment and personality.

Mature love is the adoration that you have for an individual and your appreciation of their inner qualities. In addition, the long-term relationship that has been built through the years is indispensable and must be cherished.

Real love is based on commitment, and the decision to share and make the best of life together. Commitment says, "I love you beyond the physical and natural, recognizing that there is a spiritual and supernatural connection as well." Commitment says, "I choose to share the rest of my life with you." Real commitment says, "With God we can do this thing called marriage." With God you and your spouse can accomplish great things together.

It is possible for a man to love his wife and get total satisfaction from who she is mentally and physically, and vice versa. Times may change, physical appearances may change, but true love *can* last forever.

LOVE YOUR ENEMIES

Scripture commands us to love our enemies. It doesn't necessarily mean you feel anything else for your enemies, but you are commanded to love them. You may feel like the person closest to you is no longer your friend (or has even become an enemy), but you must love them. Enemies are necessary. Allow others' hatred to breed determination; and realize that hatred exists because you have something valuable to offer and people recognize it. Mediocre people are never intimidating. Make a choice not to allow feelings of jealousy or hatred to creep up in you. Until you make the choice to stop hating on another person's success, you will never experience the great things that could be in your life. Hatred is a hindrance, so choose not to hate, but celebrate!

LOVE: MORE THAN A FEELING

According to God, love is more than a feeling—it is a choice. Keep the mentality that Jesus (our perfect example) set on the cross: to the people that inflicted His pain, His words were, "Father, forgive them for they don't know what they are doing." That's love. After all, God is love, and if you've got God, you've got love. God has given each of us the capacity to love others as He loves us: unconditionally.

TYPES OF LOVE

The bible describes several types of love:

- phileo, or familial love

- eros, or erotic love

- agape, or unconditional love

- storge, communal love

When someone does not understand the meaning of true love, conflict arises. The end result is a troubled relationship. Remember: love is a commandment and a choice.

SOUL POWER

There are two components to your soul:

1. Your will

2. Your emotion

Your will should always rule over your emotions and not the other way around. According to scripture, those who let their emotions rule over their life are "weak willed"

A million times in your life you are going to like doing something you shouldn't do, but in those times, your will has to rule over your emotions. Your will has to say, "You can't say that," or, "You can't do that." If you allow Him, God will superimpose

His will over your will. In order for that to happen, you must yield your feelings and emotions to the will of God and embrace that God is Lord over your life.

RESPONSIBLE WILL

You have to subject your feelings to God and a *responsible* will. Make a choice to be a responsible person: a decision that only God can help you with.

When your emotions are in control, you don't care how others feel. But your *God directed* will can overpower those emotions and, in turn, allow you to care. You must make a decision to care for others and realize that relationships are not built on luck, fate or chemistry . . .they are a choice.

THE VOICE

In my young life, I had strong parental guidance, and I am thankful for that. Maybe a parent or an individual had a wonderful impact and you didn't want to disappoint them. On the other hand, maybe you didn't have anyone like that at all. Wherever you are, the fact that you are reading this book means that God has sustained you and never left you alone. The fact is, your best days and your best decisions are ahead of you.

Before my relationship with God, and before I could actually hear God's voice, I loved my parents so much and feared the consequences of making bad decisions. I would think twice before doing something and could actually hear the reprimanding tone of my father's voice and see the disappointment in my mother's eyes. It was real for me, and it helped keep me on track.

As parents, we should realize that before our children reach a point of decision to accept Christ in their lives (as their personal savior), you are the example and the face of disappointment. As children grow and mature, (with time) they develop a personal relationship with God for themselves.

When you get to the point in life where you are ready to embrace a personal relationship with God, you will have access to Godly direction. This Godly direction will exemplify what I previously described with my parents. Accountability to parental authority (leadership). As you grow spiritually, you will mature and decipher the difference between the "voice of truth" and the "voice of pure deception".

Throughout life, you will always be faced with "two voices" and "two choices": good or bad, right or wrong.

"My sheep hear my voice, and I know them, and they follow me:" (John 10:27 KJV)

The Bible also says that God prefers us to be "hot or cold", because if one is luke-warm, God will spew you out of His mouth. In other words, God is saying "Don't be wishy-washy! You are either good or bad, right or wrong." There is no middle ground. Make the right choice and weigh out your decisions before you react.

Point

Kingdom living is black and white. No more gray.

Expectations

God expects that we live a life that is full of truth, confidence and integrity. The heart of God towards us is pure and true.

God expects that you recognize *who* you are and have a sense of direction in your life. Don't continue life as a wanderer with no sense of direction. Make a tough decision, and stand *on* and *up* for righteousness, and stand by it.

Some decisions may be tougher than others, but when you hear from God, stand by what God says. If God is saying nothing at all, stand still and continue to pray. Keep the communication line open and wait on God's guidance and direction. Embrace the power of God, and it will lead, guide and direct you into all truth.

HOW DO YOU KNOW THE VOICE OF GOD?

This may not make sense to you, but when I am asked, I describe the voice of God like this:

The voice of God is that calm, quiet, but stern voice of correction that always gives you the right guidance.

The loud, hasty, rushed, panicky voice is not the voice of God. If it seems on the spur of the moment or if there is no regard for the outcome of your actions, it is not God. That voice is of the enemy.

The closer you are to God and the stronger your relationship becomes, the better you will know His (God's) voice. In the natural sense, when my husband speaks,

I'm so connected that I can pick his voice out of a crowd. I could be blindfolded in a strange room and I would know his voice. How much more with God?

"MOKEY" AND "SMOKEY"

Everything the devil tells you is not true. If you hear a voice telling you that you are nothing and will never accomplish your dreams, then you know immediately that it isn't the truth and it didn't come from God. God has a divine purpose and positive plan for your life. He instructs and guides you to what is right and those things that will get you closer to your destiny.

Recognize that we all have a "Mokey" and a "Smokey" that go at it all day. One says, "You can do it! Be confident!" and the other says, "You can't do this. You are weak and inept." One wreaks havoc and keeps you in constant fear of failure, the other says "You are the greatest, and you will win."

When you hear that negative voice, listen to God and work harder to accomplish your goals. You can overpower all of the negative voices in your life through God.

A good rule to apply is this:

Everything the devil tells you is not true. It's a lie. Flip it around and begin to speak and declare the opposite, until you begin to walk in your destiny. It's time to make a decision to overcome *self-defeat* and negative *self-talk*.

MY STORY, PART FIVE- GROWING UP

Growing up, I always thought about the consequences before I acted. I'm not saying I was perfect and if I could go back and do some things differently, I would. Overall, though, I was always the kind of child to think, "Now if I do that, what is going to happen?"

Even when I was thinking about getting married, I weighed out the consequences. Don and I formed a very tight friendship before we had thoughts of actually dating. After I felt a release from God, we started to date.

Throughout the dating process, I was collecting information, praying and considering the consequences. I considered my age: I was 22 years young at the time!

We each prayed and asked God if we were making the right decision to marry so young. Everything seemed so right with us. We were in love, but the fact that neither of us had really pursued a serious relationship before and were virgins meant we wanted to make sure we were ready for a lifelong commitment.

TIP: Dating is not a time to "try out" your prospective spouse. It is really an evaluation period. Ladies: don't give away all the goods before you know if the man is worthy of the prize.

Don and I wanted to make sure that the decision we made would be for life. We had to take time, and quiet moments to listen, pray and observe, before moving into such an important union. *Marriage.*

It is important to stop, take time out for prayer and consecration, and observe where you are and where you want to be in life before making a major decision.

We get so busy that we don't have time for faith, and we want to make things happen fast, but take a second and breathe. Take time to rest in God and allow Him to talk to you in that still, small voice. Its time not only to make *good choices-but great choices.*

MAKE GREAT CHOICES

- Here are a few:
- Choose to love God.
- Choose to love yourself.
- Choose to love others.
- Choose to love life itself.
- Choose to forgive.
- Make a choice to follow Gods specific plan for your life.
- Choose happiness

In most circumstances, our nature is to love and be loved, but I want to challenge you to make a choice to love God's way: to love in spite of everything and give love even if it isn't reciprocated. Make a choice to give love, and whatever you need will in turn be given to you.

> For God so loved the world, that he gave his only begotten Son, that whosoever believeth in him should not perish, but have everlasting life. (John 3:16 KJV)

God's voice and His choice for you are good. Let that knowledge rule you. It is God's will that I prosper and win, and I have all that I need to walk into my destiny and live a successful and prosperous life.

Let's start making *good* choices and thinking things through. Stop, look, pray, and listen. I encourage everyone to make the conscious effort to make *good* decisions. It is always a good practice to weigh out the *good* and the bad before reacting.

The Bible promises that if we acknowledge Him (God) in all of our ways, He has promised that He will direct our path.

THE BLAME GAME IS OVER

Our lives are the summation of our choices. Stop playing the blame game. Look back over everything you have done, and if you're honest you will realize any failures or regrets are simply no one else's fault but yours.

You may be saying, "You don't know what they did to me," or "You don't know what happened."

You have to "own" your story and take the power out of the enemies' hands... get over it! It's time to move forward into your future.

When you own your story and take responsibility for your actions, you will stop the victim mentality. Examine a person who always blames other people for their downfall or mistakes. In some cases, they are depressed and unfulfilled, always shifting the blame, and therefore unhappy.

It's time to get up, do something about your situation and stop the blame game. A mature mind says, "I am responsible and accountable for my decisions." Will you continue to allow self-pity and pain to dominate your life? Or will you pull yourself up out of the pit and prepare yourself for the palace? God's voice and His choice for you is good. Let that rule you and stop blaming others for your decisions. They are not responsible for your actions. You are!!

EXERCISE
TRY THIS

When faced with a tough decision, continue to pray, but also do the following:

- Identify a decision that needs to be made.

- Grab a sheet of paper, cell phone or computer and title it with the important decision.

Example:

Should I accept the promotion and move?

- Create two columns;

- 1 (Pros): write down the possible and definite **positive** outcomes that will occur from making this decision. Be sure to include the best possible thing that could happen.

- 2 (Cons): write down the possible and definite **negative** outcomes that will occur from making this decision. Be sure to include the worst possible thing that could happen.

- Take a couple of days and continue to think about and write down the pros and cons of the decision that come to mind.

- After prayer, and when you feel you have gotten everything down, tally up each column.

- Before your eyes you will see that one significantly outweighs the other. If it doesn't, you will still feel a strong positive response to one column over the other. Does reading the pros column make taking the promotion and moving away feel exciting and achievable? Or sick to the stomach? Then you have your answer.

With a mature mindset, evaluate the results with people you love and trust. Share your decision with them and be open to discussion.

I find that with prayer and this type of practical, intelligent thinking, making some of the most critical decisions that I have had to make in life have been made simpler.

Along life's journey make good, sound, and mature choices. Lean on your God-given gift of discernment. Stay close to God so that when He speaks, you won't be too far away to hear Him.

Pros	Cons
_____	_____
_____	_____
_____	_____
_____	_____
_____	_____
_____	_____
_____	_____
_____	_____
_____	_____
_____	_____
_____	_____
_____	_____
_____	_____
_____	_____
_____	_____
_____	_____
_____	_____
_____	_____
_____	_____
_____	_____
_____	_____
_____	_____

SIT DOWN, SHUT UP AND LISTEN

There comes a time in each of our lives that we must sit down, quiet ourselves and listen. The more we quiet ourselves and look to God for guidance and direction, the better our lives will be. It's time to shut up the noise, get to a quiet place in God and listen.

Many times we become so busy that we have no time to hear from nor communicate with God. We no longer take time to pray, read our Bible and spend quality time with God. No longer are we concerned with finding balance between church and family. We have become busy doing what amounts to nothing... in a hurry to go nowhere. We must never forget to honor God and slow down long enough to listen to Him.

TIME OUT!!

When a young child has a tantrum, the grownup in the room must take control of the situation. Outside of what the child is trying to express, there is an opportunity for them to learn and grow. I call these special times, "teachable moments." Parents deal with outbursts in different ways. Many parents use the timeout method, removing the child from the situation and placing them in a corner of a room or somewhere quiet to think about their actions and calm down.

On the flip side, mothers of old had a way of talking to children when they wanted to get their attention. It was direct and strong, and when they said something there was no doubt in the child's mind that they had better listen and straighten up.

My mother would give me 'The Eye'. That *eye* was enough to make me behave immediately; she wouldn't have to say one word. I knew that if her eye squinted, next would come the finger. Once *the finger* pointed and *the eye* squinted, I was in big trouble!

I am so happy to say that as the baby of my family *the eye* and *the finger* were enough to save me from ever getting a spanking.

LISTEN AND LEARN

There are times when we are caught up in believing that we have all of the answers, and that we can handle everything by ourselves. It's actually just the opposite. Relax and recognize that you may not have all of the answers, all of the time.

Young children go through a phase where they don't want help with anything. They want to put on their own clothes, eat their food (their way), and walk on their own with no assistance.

As the grownup or parent, we have to step back and let them try to do it by themselves. We know that if they would just accept our help, they could be done with what occupies them and have moved on to something else. This is not the point. The point is to allow them to grow, learn and act for themselves.

When they do need assistance, it doesn't mean that they are incapable, it just means that they need to pause for a minute, listen and learn. When they listen, we can understand what we need from each other. It is when we stop and listen that we gain the insight necessary to conquer the most difficult times in our lives.

I have learned during the quiet, still and peaceful times to embrace precious, life-changing experiences. It is in the still of the storm or during a quiet time of consecration that God speaks clearest. Then it is in our times of meditation that we learn the heart of God. We must listen to God first, and then listen to others in whom we have confidence.

Have you ever started something new and reached a point where you weren't making progress or even, try as you might, you couldn't get started at all? These are the times when a little help goes a long way. The help, prayers and encouragement of the right people can catapult you towards another level of your success. An encouraging word can give someone the strength to carry on, and a listening ear might be the remedy to a problem. When you learn to accept help from people, you can then know how best to offer it to others. Can you be that shoulder to lean on when someone is in trouble? It begins with listening and learning.

SETTLE YOURSELF

Life is busy and we run so much that we rarely have time to settle down. Recognize that it is important to take time to bring positive change into your life. When we are constantly talking and busy, we do not hear the plan of God, let alone find ourselves in a position to hear what those close to us have to say that could help us.

Our generation is constantly busy, and constantly in touch with the world twenty-four hours a day . . . the Internet, television and cell phones. There is no 'off switch' on any of these devices. The current social media age is hopping, live, twenty-four-seven! It is never ending, and this poses a major problem.

Recently, my family went to dinner and I realized that instead of verbally communicating with each other, every one of us was on their cell phone (including me), locked onto our own screen. When we realized that we were not communicating with each other, we put our cell phones away and began to engage in meaningful conversation.

In today's society, there are many distractions. We post pictures of our every move, 'check in' at our location, share where and what we eat, and how we feel emotionally in the moment. In emotional outbursts, we post to get someone's sympathy and attention. In times past, we would find someone to talk to in those tender times, but now we reach for our phones and social media. As a matter of fact, when we wake up in the morning, the first thing most of us reach for is our cell phone. Before we go to bed at night, our last glance is often at a text or an email that we have received.

I believe that there are positives to social media so long as it is used in good taste and moderation. Social media can be a great tool to encourage positive action, get information out quickly, and evangelize.

It's scary that our children can live and communicate in a world and enter into friendships with strangers that we know nothing about.

> **Point**
>
> Never replace verbal communication and "a personal touch" with text, emails and social media. Keep a certain personal connection.

Because social media shuts the parent out with secret passcodes, etc., parents are becoming distanced from their children's lives. It's good to put down the phone, step into the family room and talk. It is also good for the parent to check out content on social media and have all pass codes of minors. Stay connected to what your child is connected to!

There are many great conversations that can happen when sitting down at the dinner table.

THE DINNER TABLE

Fellowship while eating dinner is now a rarity.

The dinner table was the time that my family had some of our most intimate talks and is definitely a time where my husband and I give sound advice, share, and pour into our children. It gives us time as a family to express ourselves and discuss things that may be troubling us. Let's slow down and reintroduce sitting down to dinner as a family at least a couple of times a week.

TALK LESS AND PRAY MORE

We are constantly busy trying to make things happen by our own will and power. In actuality the thing that we are working so hard to accomplish may simply not come to be. It becomes wasted effort when we strive to no end.

Never force something. Trying to make it work at all costs can cost a person's family, spouse or loved ones and it's simply not worth it. Count your losses and move on.

In some of the most trying times in my life, when a critical decision had to be made, I slowed down, quieted myself, talked less and prayed a lot more. I can recall those defining moments in my life when God gave me clear direction about what to do and how to do it. There were times when I got clear-cut direction, stopped praying and took it from there, only to make a mess. I learned to stay committed and connected to God through the whole process.

Be realistic with yourself and your situation and remember that whatever you can't talk about. you can definitely pray about. Talk less and pray more.

WHO TALKS MORE? MEN OR WOMEN?

Some studies say women are more talkative than men. Depending on the source, some say that women talk more than twice as much as men: 20,000 words a day for women, 7,000 a day for men. †

Between male and female, there are times when we don't take the time to listen to what is being said, or we let our emotions take over. We should make a practice of active listening.

Have you ever had a conversation with someone and it is obvious that the person you are talking to isn't really listening? It becomes evident that as soon as you finish, they start up a different conversation or make a statement that has nothing to do with the current subject matter. You know that they have just been waiting for their turn to talk and basically ignored everything that you've said. Have you ever been talked over by someone? It's not a good feeling. Or has someone ever asked you a question that was directed to you personally but another person has chimed in and answered the question that was directed to you? That's rude.

Point

Effective communication is a relay and exchange of words
and a two-way conversation. It may consist of listening, but at
times it is the ability to engage in sharing and receiving.

I know that at some time or another we have all experienced a person who would not quiet down for a minute and use etiquette when communicating. This type of poor communication can occur at home, in the workplace, in a marriage, a friend-ship; or between adults or children.

It is never a good feeling to be ignored by the person you are talking to. Make sure you do not make others feel this way by listening attentively.

> **Point**
>
> When engaging in active communication, stop and listen and show interest in what the other individual is saying. You would be surprised to see how effective of a communicator you can be by simply taking time out to listen.

Communication Within the Family

When children are young, communication with them is quite easy. As they grow, however, there will come a time when children may not tell their parents everything, especially when they become teenagers.

I remember when my children were younger. Every day, I would ask them questions: "How was school?" or "How was your day?" My husband and I learned a lot by talking and listening. We communicated about everything we could possibly think of, including sex, relationships, and anything else that was on their minds. We started this early, so that when they got to their teen years, it was just a part of our regular routine.

Under current societal pressures, we have to prepare ourselves to answer tough questions, and sometimes pray for those answers. When it comes to modern gender and sexuality, adults have to prepare to have intense conversations with our children. We must brace ourselves for the current day, complicated issues. Times have changed, and the dialogue that we must now have is totally different than it was when I grew up. There is definitely a need for mature conversation early on.

Parents, as our children grow older, our role will change from that of *telling* to *offering* advice. We should value our children's opinions and let them choose whether to accept what we tell them. After we offer our opinion and what we feel it is their best option, we have to pray for wisdom as to how we will gently guide them into making the right choices. As adults, we need to show a level of maturity and listen to our children, as they may not always agree. Realize that they can bring you another perspective.

SHUT DOWN MODE: A TOOL FOR HUSBANDS AND WIVES

"Shut Down mode" is not what you might think. It is not silent treatment. It's about getting quiet, taking a vacation, or simply sitting and talking. In other words, it's about changing the context of a difficult situation in order to improve it. My husband Pastor Don and I will take time to go to a coffee shop, just the two of us, and talk about what we want to accomplish or what challenges we are facing. We share priceless information along with what we need the other's prayer for. It has always been so refreshing to know that I can unload with my hubby, who is my best friend in the entire world.

Don genuinely cares: he loves me unconditionally and wants the best for my life. I know Don will give good advice or a listening ear and a shoulder to lean on. You can get a lot done when you shut down from everything else in your relationship and take time to communicate.

We can really botch things up when we are always in a hurry. It's so important to listen with your heart. Don't be so busy that one day you wake up and all your children are grown and you are left with a spouse that has become a total stranger. It is disheartening to realize that all of those years that you invested in your children, has resulted in separation with your spouse. When you don't take the time to nurture your relationship, with each day you will find yourself growing distant from your spouse. It will be sad to find that while you were filling your children up with love and support that your relationship has been left empty. Plan now to spend valuable time with your spouse and invest in your marriage beyond your children's presence in the home.

BE THE VILLAGE

Don and I started our family a year after we got married. I didn't have much time to learn anything, so I would constantly lean on God for direction and guidance. He gave me great advice because I had to quiet down, open my ears and listen.

God always gives great wisdom, if you would open up and listen.

When my husband was called to be a pastor, I wanted to be the best "First Lady" ever. But I got caught up in trying to be the epitome of a "perfect" First Lady. I remember it like it was yesterday; I felt alone and helpless. I didn't know the first thing about being a pastor's wife, and here was another level of responsibility added to my other obligations.

Finally, after days of contemplating my next move, I mustered up enough strength to pick up the phone and call someone whom I looked up to and admired. Well, I called for what I thought would be a listening ear of compassion and advice, only to be rejected and hurt. They were appalled that I would ask them for advice. They told me that they had nothing to say, and hung up the phone.

I dropped the receiver, ran into the living room, fell on the floor and began to cry. I was in a different place, embarking on a journey that I knew nothing about.

My two-year-old son (Don III), walked over, and I felt a tap on my shoulder. I looked up and stopped crying for a moment. He said, "Mom, what are you crying for? Mom, get up and dry your eyes, the Lord is with you!"

I looked up in amazement; here was this two-year- old baby, talking to me like a thirty-year-old man! There was such maturity in his voice and I knew it came from God. Don III helped me up and I lifted my hands and looked towards heaven.

Then the voice of the Lord spoke to me and said, "You will now walk this journey as a Pastor's wife. I will guide you and you will listen."

God continued, "The reason why no one can advise you on how to be a pastor's wife is because you are mine and you will be a replica of "no one". I will guide you and from this day forward you will listen to my voice and my voice alone."

I can truly say that I have stopped, listened and depended on God from that day forward.

In the middle of the chaos, God spoke to me through my son. I stopped my *pity party* and moved forward with courage and confidence.

My husband's direction from God was to start a ministry, and as a watchman of God's people, I knew Don could bring clarity to my experience that day.

I decided to ask Don what he desired as far as my ministry to the people to whom God had entrusted in our care. I asked my hubby how I could help him build ministry, and from that day forward, I have listened to God, and my husband (whom I know hears from God directly). If I had NOT shut up and listened to my two-year-old son—and therefore God—that day, I don't know where I would be today.

HANG UP THE PHONE

As time went on I had two more children, Courtney and Andrea. Wow! Three children, a Pastor's wife, and a new ministry that we were building from the ground up. I also worked afternoons in emergency and was finishing my college degree at the same time.

My husband was working around the clock (he worked three jobs at the time) to take care of our family. I prayed that God would bless my hubby with a single job that would take care of the family, and a week later he received a call from an automotive company that would earn him more money than all three jobs combined, and his shift was opposite mine. Our opposite schedules worked out so that we wouldn't have to pay a babysitter.

Each day I had the same routine: get up, make breakfast, bathe and dress the children, nap time, story time and make dinner before I went to work. My desire was to settle everything before my shift so that it would be easier for Don to take care of the children in the evening once he got off work.

One particular day, I woke up to begin my daily routine. I got everyone breakfast and that is when things got a little out of hand. The phone rang constantly, one call after another, with little things that people of our congregation could have handled themselves. Time moved on and I was still talking on the phone. I looked up at the clock. It was 2:30 and my shift started at 3:00. I was frantic: I had prepared no dinner, the children weren't dressed and I had spent my entire day talking on the phone to *needy* congregants. I ran into my room and God stopped me in my tracks and said, "Sit down and listen. I have something to say."

I sat down on my bed, head turned sideways, hands on my chin, and looked up at the ceiling. I felt like saying, "God, you know I'm already late . . . can we get this conversation over with?"

The Lord said, "Don't ever neglect your children or your family to talk on the phone."

God went on to say, "The members of the congregation will be okay and you can't be a mother and wife if they cause you to neglect your responsibility. "Help the congregation to understand that you are a young mom with small children who require your undivided attention. Explain, that you work every day."

I felt bad, and I was convicted by God's word; after all, the biblical principle is that charity starts at home I took this scripture to heart.

I looked up towards heaven and said, "I'm listening."

I went to work and felt so bad afterwards, but I had learned through this experience to quiet my fears, talk to God and listen for instruction.

His Word was, "Don't get so busy that you neglect your family."

When we are in the right place, God will send whoever or whatever He needs to speak to us. God wants to bring definition and clarity to those things that you may not have answers for.

DISCERNMENT AND PERSONAL CONVICTION

Discernment and motherly instinct are the greatest tools in childrearing. God will give everyone their own set of instructions to help them reach their individual and personal destiny. This is what I deem to be a "personal conviction." Discernment means to judge well.

MY STORY, PART SIX PERSONAL CONVICTION

I had a personal conviction. God gave me instruction, and I stuck to it. Many times outside of my local church I have been ridiculed, misunderstood and looked upon as non-participatory.

There were even those who felt that I was selfish and only cared about my husband, my church, and my family. The question then was: please people or please God?

I choose God all day and every day. I took the criticism because I knew what God said, and I knew my husband's expectations for his family, therefore I had to close my ears to the "dumb stuff" and continue on.

I advise you to start today to develop your personal relationship with God. Listen for *His* voice and instructions, and stop trying to hear God through other people's opinions. Clear the line and follow God.

Even now that my children are grown, God encourages me to never remove myself from the commitment and time that it takes to care for my family and ministry. I have great compassion for young moms with babies, but I encourage them to remember that their children won't be babies forever, so they should invest their time, impart morals and standards, and—most importantly—pour the love of Jesus into their children's hearts. I also encourage them to seek God and pray for Him to reveal their personal conviction. After they receive that conviction, they should move forward unconcerned with people who don't get it; many of them never will.

If you are reading this book, I believe you are ready to change. Ask God for personal guidance and the strength to carry out His plan for your life. God has a set of specific instructions that will keep you on schedule to the fulfillment of your destiny.

EXERCISE
TIME TO REFLECT

Take time to recall and write about a moment when you sat down, shut up and listened to God. Write down your personal conviction.

_____

_____

_____

_____

_____

_____

_____

_____

_____

_____

_____

_____

_____

_____

_____

_____

_____

_____

_____

_____

_____

Point

The key to hearing from God is simple: listen, learn, and respond.

EXERCISE
THE COMMUNICATION LIST

Name five things you could do to become a better communicator with God and others.

-

_____

-

_____

-

_____

-

_____

-

_____

A BETTER PLACE

How can we get to a better place in our lives? Start by following these steps.

Step One: Take Ownership

In order to get to a better place, you must admit to the place you are in. Take ownership and embrace the fact that you may have messed up in the past and failed to listen (whether to God or your loved ones). By reading this book, you have already started to take ownership.

Step Two: Acknowledge

Acknowledge that you can do nothing without God's voice and direction in your life. He has created a master plan to help you reach your ordained purpose, but you must acknowledge that plan and follow it. There may be times when you take a detour, but you must get back on track and begin moving towards your victory. Realize that God is omnipresent: God is with you, ahead of you, and He knows everything about you. Your destiny is controlled by God, but your future is in your hands. Will you follow God's strategy for your success?

Step Three: Ask for Forgiveness

You may be saying to yourself, "But you don't know what I did!" or "You don't know what they did to me!"

You can forgive without forgetting. Remember that God is great at forgiving us, no matter how horrible things may seem. You cannot hear from God clearly when you hold onto anger and guilt. Clear the line and forgive yourself and others.

Remember that forgiveness is available to anyone who understands that grace is due to everyone. Recognize that nobody's perfect—and that includes you!

This also means you must forgive yourself. Many people carry past hurt and pain and hold onto the guilt of their past. Let it go and move on!

Step Four: Make a Plan and Put It in Motion.

As we've discussed earlier in this book, you must write down your plan of action and begin the process of strategically positioning yourself for victory.

There is a release that comes with making a plan and committing it to paper. Success may not come overnight, but be patient and willing to keep at it, and you will achieve your desired result.

Step Five: Settle and Quiet yourself

Reflect and listen to others and you will discover that when you are a good listener, your overall communication skills improve. I might add that your relationships will grow stronger when you become a great listener.

Take time each day to cherish the quiet times in life. These are the moments when you can sit down, listen, and explore fresh perspectives. God is the best at listening to everything you want to share, and you can talk to God and know that you can trust Him with your deepest secrets. As you talk to God, the exchange of information will be amazing, and you will experience relief and freedom. Give your heart totally to Him and in turn you will receive wisdom and revelatory knowledge that will help you to pursue your wildest dreams. Stop, 'Shut Down', shut up, and listen!

8 TWO SERVANTS IN LOVE

POWER IN PARTNERSHIP

There is power in partnership:

> 9 Two are better than one; because they have a good reward for their labour.
>
> 10 For if they fall, the one will lift up his fellow: but woe to him that is alone when he falleth; for he hath not another to help him up. (Ecclesiastes 4:9-10)

Marriage is a partnership and there are several components that make a successful marriage. A God designed marriage is between two people (husband and wife) who commit to living life as **one**. Marriage is a close-knit relationship between a man and woman, in which they work together to bring glory to God through their union.

My husband Don and I are committed to continually growing each day. Our heartfelt desire is to build a great marriage. We have made a choice to stay together through good and bad, ups and downs.

Through it all, we have kept God first, and in tough times we trust in God's plan for our marriage. He never fails to show grace and mercy towards both of us.

OUR STORY

Don and I had both been raised in God-fearing homes. We learned early on that we had to trust in God and each other every step of the way.

From the start, we made up our minds to model our life as in *two servants* love. We vowed that we would make each other our main objective and not worry selfishly about our individual needs alone. Don promised that he would take care of my needs and I promised to take care of his. We realized that if we operated by this principle that we would always prefer one another in all things. (Taking care of the children will be automatic.)

A marriage should be between two spiritually *whole* people who come together to create something that has never existed before. You may have heard one person tell another, "You complete me." Sorry, but I believe that in order for marriage to work, both parties must be complete(whole) to begin with. No one wants a "half-baked" person.

Anyone who desires a normal and healthy marriage should desire to marry someone who is whole, purpose driven and confident in who they are before God.

Becoming complete in one's self simply means understanding the real power of becoming a servant. It is important that you are never domineering over your spouse; true servanthood is in the power to work together towards a common goal. It is not power-tripping!

Don and I work together in ministry, in parenthood, and as spouses. We are partners and support one another, not only in personal endeavors, but also in the professional and spiritual endeavors. It is understood within our congregation that my husband and I are on the *same page* and of one accord. We have never allowed anyone to separate us. People will try, even members of the congregation will try, but we stay close and speak the same thing!

Point

Husbands and Wives stand strong and stand together...As one.

I serve Don, and he serves me. We are happily married, in sync, united as one, together.

My job, mission and heart's desire, is to make sure that Donny has what he desires as he does for me. This is the kind of unselfish love every woman deserves and the love that every man needs.

> Husbands, love your wives, even as Christ also loved the church, and gave himself for it;
>
> (Ephesians 5:25 KJV)

Man is commanded to love his wife as he loves himself and as Christ loved the church.

What did Christ do that exemplified His love?

The answer is clear: he died for the church, which symbolizes the un-compromising and unselfish love that Christ gives to each of us…daily.

A man who loves his wife will cherish her and treat her with honor and respect. A man should honor his wife so much that he won't do anything to purposefully hurt her. Neither will he abuse his "better half," either verbally or physically.

SUBMISSION IS NOT SIMPLICITY

Many people have the wrong perception of *submission*. The word "submission" gets a bad rap and some people think that it means inequality or subservience. Submission is not exclusively a woman's role in marriage, but true submission goes both ways and applies to both husband and wife.

While the husband is the head of the house, he is also commanded to love, honor and respect the woman God gives to him.

> But I would have you to know, that the head of every man is Christ; and the head of the woman is the man; and the head of Christ is God. (I Corinthians 11:3 KJV)

The bible clearly lets us know where the responsibility lies concerning submission. It is not lop-sided but it is dual.

> Submitting yourselves one to another in the fear of God. (Ephesians 5:21 KJV)

Most women willfully submit to a "real" man, and when you have a husband that fears God and loves his family, submission comes easy. It's when a man does not provide for his family or set a good example that it becomes hard for his wife, and at times his children, to follow.

Many women cringe at the word "submission." Submission does not mean that you lose your identity and self-worth. Submission does mean that you are not only confident in who you are, but it does mean that you honor and respect the authority of your husband. When you love your spouse and submit to them, your desire is to help them reach their destiny and revere God in the process.

> Wives, submit yourselves unto your own husbands, as unto the Lord. (Ephesians 5:22 KJV)

If a woman finds herself submitting to anyone else more than she submits to her husband, it's time to evaluate. If she finds herself submitting to her male boss or men in the church more than she submits to her husband, then it's time to consider why.

I am grateful that Don and I have no issue when it comes to preferring/honoring one another (over all others). We made a decision to never allow people to come between us. Our marriage is never a "power struggle". I know who my husband is and understand his role in our family. Pastor Don is my hubby, my best friend and confidant. He is an awesome man of God, and on top of that, he is my Pastor, the priest of my home and my shepherd.

Point

Honor and respect are very important in marriage.

A "God-fearing" husband reveres the fact that without God there is no plan. He has a "good head" on his shoulders, or in other words, the care and compassion that Christ has for the church is the same care that a husband should give to his wife. Christ is head of the church, and the man is head of the wife. The man cannot lead effectively if he has not accepted Christ as his head. If he rejects Christ as the head of his life and rejects guidance, he is in turn a 'headless man'. No one wants to follow a "headless man".

Again, it isn't hard to submit to someone who has goals, dreams and a vision. When both parties have each other's best interests at heart and open up their hearts to God, they will automatically lose their selfish pride, and in turn honor what the Bible says.

THE THIRD STRAND

A three-stranded cord is not easily broken. What is the common thread that holds every marriage together? It is the third strand—God. A marriage is fortified and strengthened when God is interwoven within. God is the third strand as well as the defining factor that will hold things together and prevents the cord from breaking. The love of Christ at the center of a marriage becomes the "balancer". Show me a solid marriage, and I'll show you two people who revere and honor God in their personal lives and in turn exemplify the love of God to everyone.

> And if one prevail against him, two shall withstand him; and a threefold cord is not quickly broken. (Ecclesiastes 4:12 KJV)

WITHOUT A VISION . . .

> Where there is no vision, the people perish: but he that keepeth the law, happy is he. (Proverbs 29:18 KJV)

It is imperative that you have a clear vision of what God has in store for your life, career, purpose, and family. Your marriage will suffer if you don't have a clear idea of who you are, what your goals are as an individual (and as a family), and what direction everyone is going in. When you receive direction from God, run with that vision.

When my husband and I counsel couples, we will ask if they have a vision and purpose for their marriage. If two people are not in agreement, they will not be in a place to serve one another, and it will become difficult to have an honest and loving relationship.

WHAT'S THE PLAN?

Important questions that my husband and I ask when counseling married or engaged couples:

1. What do you want to accomplish together as husband and wife?

2. What are your individual goals?

3. What are your collective long-term goals?

4. If there are children in the house, do they understand the family's goals, and do they have goals of their own?

5. Do you each feel secure and confident in your partner's love?

6. Are you willing to revere God and put him first?

EXERCISE
THE GREAT MENTOR

Read -Ruth 1:14-17

Read- II Kings 2:1-12

_____

_____

_____

_____

_____

_____

_____

_____

_____

_____

_____

_____

_____

_____

_____

_____

_____

_____

_____

_____

_____

_____

_____

_____

The bible has several examples of mentor/mentee relationships. The ultimate example of one that leads by example is Jesus. Jesus is our perfect example and every day we are striving to exemplify the characteristics of His life. Elisha looked to his mentor Elijah for direction and counsel for his life. Elisha's desire was to receive a "double portion" of Elijah's spirit. This is one of the greatest examples of a mentor-mentee relationship. We can also find an example of exemplary mentorship in the relationship between Ruth and Naomi.

Ruth told Naomi that "I will go where you go, lodge where you lodge and your people will be my people." In the end Ruth was blessed beyond measure because she stuck by Naomi and followed her instruction.

Whether you are a wife, mother, or daughter, you must take time to develop a personal relationship with God to find out what God's ultimate and specific plan is for your life. After you have sought the plan of God, then execute it by seeking out a good mentor who leads by example and clearly represents the direction in which you are headed.

THE POWER OF AGREEMENT

There is power in partnership and there is power in agreement. Husbands and wives don't pull against each other; they should work together and pull in the same direction.

That does not mean that you have to be exactly the same, because you will never be the same two people. Realize that you cannot change your spouse. Ladies, your husband needs a wife, not a mother. You cannot 'retrain' your adult husband. The last thing you want to do is degrade your husband's character and masculinity by treating him like a child.

Example: Your husband is at the dinner table with friends, engaged in conversation. As he speaks, you sigh and act as if everything he says is absurd or dumb. Ladies, never, ever embarrass your spouse—in public or even in private. I mention 'in private' because if you make a practice of respecting one another in private, your respect will automatically show in public.

Never treat your husband like a child, even though you are a nurturer by nature. As husband and wife, you can confidently appreciate and embrace each other's similarities and differences. Then together, become the man and woman that God wants you to be, as individuals and as a family.

On the flip-side, men never treat your wife like a child. Respect her as your "lady of the house", and try hard to make her feel like "your queen". Don't flex your muscles and constantly in a domineering way remind her that you don't have to listen to her because you are in charge.

When a husband and wife work together, encouraging and investing one in the other, God gets the glory out of their union. Marriage is God's glorious church. Marriage is not two people on a "power-trip."

OPEN UP YOUR HEART

I want to take a moment to deal with the issues of the heart. This section is dedicated to helping every man, woman, boy or girl who reads this open up his or her heart and trust again. It is our instinctive nature to guard our hearts. Depending upon your upbringing, you may have been raised in a *guarded* family. As a child, my family of six was a close-knit family, and growing up I thought that there was absolutely no safety outside of my family. This is not necessarily a bad thing.

I was raised to love my family unconditionally. Feeling safe at home and knowing that your mom, dad, and siblings love you unconditionally is a good feeling.

It can become a bad thing, if you take this to the extreme. Never allow yourself to mistake this safety at home to equal danger outside of the home. Do not become caged and imprisoned with the thought that you have to always guard yourself from the world outside your immediate family.

I actually felt that way: that outside of my immediate family, absolutely no one could be trusted, and no one else could love and protect me like my family.

I had a defining moment when I met Donny. At first, I moved with extreme caution, not because I had been hurt by the opposite sex personally, but because of what I had witnessed in so many others who experienced betrayal. I saw hurt, abandonment and depression stem from these relationships, and I vowed that it would never be me.

I moved at a slow pace; Don and I finally begin to date after five years of knowing each other. I felt my heart opening up and I admit, it was an uncomfortable feeling at first. All of a sudden, upon opening my heart to Don, I felt vulnerable and unprotected.

One day, I was at home in prayer and the Lord revealed Don's heart to me. When we were dating, I kept a part of my heart on reserve so that if Don left, I would be able to function and not lose control, nor lose my sanity. I must add that, as I teach so many women, it is good to keep some of your heart on reserve until you say, "I do." After "I do," your heart should be completely and totally open and given away.

Always remember who has your heart first—and that never changes—God. Keep everything in proper perspective.

I have ministered to many women who are married and for a plethora of reasons, whether it be hurt, distrust, infidelity or betrayal, they withhold a part of their heart from their spouse.

In other words, they are guarded in the relationship and never open up freely; they are reserved. Therefore, the relationship never blossoms fully because of distrust.

It is a real issue when a spouse has violated trust. They must realize that it will not only take the grace of God, but it will also take trusting God for wisdom and knowledge in how to rebuild trust. The main goal for the adulterer should be to assure their spouses of their commitment to their marriage. Patience will be key and definitely a necessary virtue when dealing with the outcomes of infidelity.

The adulterer must also realize that in order to rebuild trust in a relationship, it will take patience, time and grace. And as the victim, who is understandably reserved because of past pain and hurts, you must remember that God wants you to open your heart, forgive as God forgives, and freely love and receive love from your spouse. Let go, and let God loosen the chains that bind the piece of your heart that you are holding onto. There is an unexplainable feeling of total freedom when you give yourself away, first to God and then to your spouse. There is a grace that will give you the power to forgive your spouse and move on. If moving on means that there was too much damage to reconcile… move on peaceably.

MY STORY, PART SEVEN MY HEART IS OPEN

Here is another defining moment in my life. My husband began pastoring and the Lord spoke to me and said, "Open your heart and know that I am guarding it. You no longer have to build a fortress around your heart."

I admit, I really didn't trust too many people at all. Members of our congregation would speak at services and say, "I love my pastor and his wife and family. I will never leave them."

They would also say, "I will be there whenever they need me."

Well here is the twist: when things went sour or when trials and tough times manifested in the church (or in their personal lives), they were nowhere to be seen. Let me encourage every Pastor's wife, mentor and business owner that may be reading this to never blame yourself or close yourself up because people leave you or your place of business. People come and people go, that's human nature. People may celebrate you today and hate you tomorrow. Never allow people's approval to dictate your self-worth or capabilities.

Realistically you know this, but let me reiterate: live your life, keep it moving and don't hold your breath waiting on someone else to set your destiny in motion. Don't wait on one particular person to validate your success, make it happen yourself. After all, people are not the key to your success, God is. Understand that people have a right to choose whatever or whomever they desire. While they play 'Spin the Wheel,' I choose to keep plugging away at my victory. I'm in the game of life to win! Remember, just like Joseph, people may take your coat, but they can't take your favor.

Point

Build on the foundation of the past, but construct and work toward your future.

God has given you a canvas, paint and paint brush, what will you create on the canvas of your life? You are the artist, use your creativity and paint something vibrant, unique and something new.

Live life each day with your God-given purpose in mind. Know that some people are "yesterday people" and they are not permitted to go into your future. They were good for that particular season.

My husband shared a golden nugget with me when we started Burning Bush International Ministries. That was to love the people when they come into my life, love and pray for them while they are at the church, and if they leave, love (and pray for) them as well. Finally, my husband encouraged me to keep an open heart to love people if they decided to come back. Through our years in ministry, my husband and I have stabilized by understanding that people may not be placed in our lives forever. They are God's people and if they uproot prematurely, God will have to assist them as they re-plant or position themselves elsewhere.

Realize that if you uproot prematurely it will be like starting over. After planted roots in a ministry, roots grow deep and because you can't see growth with the "naked eye", you may uproot at the time when there may have been fruit to bear. The other thing to think about is this, when a person leaves a ministry mad, upset or aggravated because things may not have gone their way, (or ministry isn't perfect), they have to be careful not to carry the offense elsewhere. The fact is there are no perfect assemblies, and there is not perfect "world or workplace for that matter.

Churches, places of employment and the. world is made up of imperfect people. I have a saying: you can move from city to city and from church to church, but wherever you go, you will take "you" along. There are no perfect church buildings, but God's church is perfected through His love and we are commissioned to build kingdom, remain resilient and be "light" in a dark world. That is why when we speak about heaven, that is he place that you will find those who lived a life in accordance to God's will.

While here on earth, deal with it, and understand that you will always face difficult people and difficult situations.

My husband says, "Don't allow people to run you out of a place that they had no power to put you in the first place." You may move to a different city, state, or church, but look up and "you" will be right there with the *same* problems and the *same* anger. You cannot blame other people. It's best to remain planted where you are and pray your way through. This is how you mature.

Over time, God may uproot and plant .as the Bible says, one plants, another waters, but God gives increase.

I recognize that I own no one, and it would be worse to try and hold onto someone who doesn't belong to me in the first place. It can be detrimental to hold onto someone that God didn't intend to remain in my life forever. I might add that God said to me, "And furthermore, for everyone that leaves (or walks away), I'm sending ten more...into your life."

Well, years later, I'm so happy to announce that if someone leaves our church, within a matter of weeks, God sends a replacement. When you honor God, He will never leave you empty and in turn fill your life up with blessings that overflow. Our total dependency should be on God and not people.

I admit that it is hard to let go of people that you genuinely pray for and love. Take comfort and know that just as we are given a free will to open our hearts to salvation, people are given that same "free will" to choose their place of worship. Our commission is to love unconditionally.

Make a declaration today and open up your heart. Love and be loved, then accept what God allows and move on.

WE CAN DO ANYTHING

I love helping people. It's just a part of who I am. In our ministry, I have the opportunity to work with young people, talk with women and, together with my husband, help families. We have a powerful ministry that is changing the lives of so many people and Don and I do it together.

In every phase of my marriage, Don has been there to support me, dating back to when I had a desire to finish my college education and Don moved to Ypsilanti, (after we got married) I had a desire to open an upscale boutique, and Don supported it. He has always supported me. When I felt the need to write this book, Don supported and encouraged it. I know he has my back and I have his. With God and my hubby, I can do anything. With God, we are a majority. Just as Don supports me in my endeavors, in turn I am his "biggest" fan and in support of his dream 100%.

NO COMPETITION HERE

Don and I experience no intimidation or confusion in our relationship. The two of us have become one, and with God's direction and help; we trust our dreams as individuals and as a family. We are confident that our dreams, individually and collectively, will come to pass.

We made a pact when we first got married to never be in competition with one another. Instead, we committed to taking care of each other, no matter what. We are together and that settles it. With God's help, no one can divide us, and together we win!

NOT 50/50

Marriage is not 50/50. Realistically there are times when things will be 40/60 or maybe even 20/80, but the key (in marriage), is to keep the final number at 100. If you to have to bear more in a particular season in your marriage, pray and ask God for the grace to minister to each other's needs. This will help both you and your spouse to keep it 100!

STICK TOGETHER

Never allow the opinions of others to create confusion in your home. Sometimes people will attempt to scare a husband into thinking their wife is against them or that they (the wife) has the desire to take over. They fail to realize that when it comes down to it, the closest relationship a man has is with his wife, and if the husband can depend on anyone, it should be her.

A "good-hearted", "God-fearing" woman will be there through thick and thin, and only desires to know that her husband trusts her. Many outsiders challenge the partnership of a husband and wife. Partnership is this: the wife understands her assignment and submission to her husband and they work together. She recognizes that her husband is the head and the final decision maker of the home. Again, not only does her husband's heart trust safely in her, her heart trusts her husband as well. At the same time, the husband understands his duty and assignment to his wife, and also his own submission to his wife, and he steps into the role of her protector and provider.

Most women who love God and trust their husbands enjoy the care, protection and covering that he gives. Personally, I love being covered and pampered by my strong and courageous husband. A lady can easily submit to her husband if he covers her. It's important she not only desires to help her husband pursue his goals and dreams, but she knows how to <u>balance</u> and pursue her own as well. As I have stated, husband and wife are helpers, one to the other, and not separate but together. There have been many days that my husband has simply held me in his arms, and the assurance of the touch of his hand and the sound of his voice saying, "It's going to be alright, I'll never let anyone hurt you," has helped me to make it through some of the most difficult times of my life. A submissive wife and a submitted/committed husband can overcome anything.

Never allow anyone or anything to come between you and your spouse, even if they are so called "spiritual." If you are a Pastor or Pastor's wife, remember to always show togetherness and be of one accord both in and out of the presence of your congregation. Never allow people to come between you and your spouse though they may try. Stay connected, cover each other and stay of one accord.

Remember that the church should edify your relationship and not tear it down. The church should see husbands and wives and their family working together. In turn, strong families are the foundation of a growing, thriving church.

These days we no longer need separation. We don't need "men's work" and "women's work", let's cultivate the mentality that *all* work is the Lord's work, and we are working together to build the Kingdom of God and reap a great harvest of souls.

TAKE COMFORT

Don loves me and covers me at home, in church, and everywhere we go. He is the kind of husband that lifts his family up and does not tear them down. I know that much of my success in ministry and the respect that I have in the church is because of my husband's adoration, respect and his validation of who I am as a lady, an evangelist, an entrepreneur, a mentor, a mother and a pastor's wife. In turn I sing Don's praises and help the congregation better understand the awesome, loving, compassionate and God-fearing shepherd who cares for them. Don is not only a dynamic leader but he is intelligent, full of vision, fearless, courageous, a mentor, and to top it off.... handsome.

Husbands and wives lift each other up and don't be ashamed to let others see your love in action. It's okay to hold hands, kiss and embrace in public. Don't throw down to the point of embarrassment, but a kiss and hand hold is appropriate for married people. You have nothing to be ashamed of. Your marriage should be the reflection of God's love here on Earth. Never perpetrate in public what never happens in private. Over time, you won't be able to "fake-it"--time will reveal truth. I watch those who go over board and say, "married-the good life", "marriage rocks", and "my boo "on social media. If you follow that couple home, they are exactly right, their marriage is "rocky", "scary" and they have much work to do on themselves and their marriage as a whole.

Strive to be the kind of couple God can trust, and let God be the center of your relationship. Ask God for an understanding of what your purpose is, and how to navigate your life in order to reach your destiny—together. Be true and prayerful in private and it will show in public without a lot of "fluff."

If you are single, start praying for the type of mate that will love God and help you reach your optimal level of success, in marriage and in life.

Ask God for direction and seek His plan, and I guarantee that when you follow God's instruction, He will lead you to ultimate victory!

9 SUBMITTED, CONVICTED AND CONNECTED

Love that is connected to the "heart of God" will cause God's word to come to life, and in turn create faith that conquers anything.

> 38 For I am persuaded, that neither death, nor life, nor angels, nor principalities, nor powers, nor things present, nor things to come,
>
> 39 Nor height, nor depth, nor any other creature, shall be able to separate us from the love of God, which is in Christ Jesus our Lord. (*Romans 8:38-39 KJV*)

My personal conviction is that, first and foremost, I will not allow anything or anyone to separate me from the love of God. It is through His love that I will experience my best life ever!

The difference between mediocrity and the extraordinary is the ability to embrace your personal conviction and stay connected with God. When the connection is lost, communication becomes difficult. Prayer is your communication with God and it is the tool with which we talk to God and express the sentiments of our heart. With no communication, there is absolutely no conviction.

If you are to excel and accomplish victory, the following questions need answers:

- What is your personal conviction?

- What path will you choose in your life? What is your calling? (Were you called to be a business owner, an educator, a nurse or doctor, a lawyer, a motivational speaker, an evangelist, or a stay at home mom?)

  Once you have identified your calling, answer these questions:

- Are you connected to God?

- Can you stay connected to God in the midst of success?

- What is your strategy?

- How will you implement your plan?

- Is God a significant part of the plan?

UNWAVERING AND UNMOVABLE

You should remain steadfast and unmovable in your conviction no matter what everyone else says or does.

If the advice given by others is contrary to what God has declared over your life, it is bad advice. When you are convicted, you will feel an insurmountable faith that no matter how long it takes, God's promises are inevitable. The promise He has made to you will appear at the right time and in the right season.

MY CONVICTION

When my husband and I got married, we vowed that we would never put one another before God. We made it clear from the start; God is first in our lives. We are convinced that if we keep God first, He will continue to guide us in all truth. Society has a way of painting women that honor God and their husbands as "weak-willed", with no goals or aspirations. Right here and right now, I want to dispel this myth.

When a woman loves her husband and her family and makes a decision to love and honor her role, she should not be viewed as a "poor", "deprived" or a "beaten" down lady with no purpose or goals.

When a woman is committed to God and her family, people feel sorry for her and make her feel as though her life has no worth. They attempt to make her feel that because she loves God first, her husband and children there is no substance or meaning to her worth. It is quite the opposite.

Point

When it comes to family values.... modern day society
views the *abnormal* as the new norm.

I want to encourage and celebrate every mother who takes the "ministry of motherhood" serious. Every "stay at home" mom: I commend you and your desire to invest in and raise your family. You are not living beneath your value.

The best investment that you will ever make is in the care and nurturing of your children and building of your home. You can find a creative way to make money, pursue your college education and work on your future goals and aspirations at the same time. The key is to never stop dreaming, nor stop moving towards the fulfillment of your purpose.

If you are a working mom and your priority is your family, I commend and celebrate you, as well.

It is not always the quantity of time, but the quality of time that's important. The concept of a "well-balanced" family is not only the amount of time spent together in a day, but rather the quality of that time and your willingness to *do* and *be* your absolute best for it.

Balance is key. The fact is that not every woman who desires to stay at home is able to because of her financial situation. It may not be the wisest decision to stay home; you have to make ends meet. Realize that whatever you have to do to make your home successful, you should do it! You are making a great investment when you take care of your responsibilities (your family). Ask God for the grace, ability and strength to make life happen. You can and will succeed.

THE STAY AT HOME MOM

"Stay at home" moms can have it all! They can pursue their goals, educational dreams and aspirations all while staying connected to their family. The "stay at home" mom is just as significant as the woman who clocks in every day at a major corporate office.

Again, society tries to make women feel that they are uneducated or ignorant if they stay at home and take care of their children. Many women feel as if they have no purpose, direction or value. But stay at home moms should be valued, not devalued!

Being the mother of five, my eyes were opened to the misguided perception of modern day society upon my decision to stay home after my third child. Families are in disarray and the chaos can be traced to mothers or fathers not being in their proper place in the home. It is important that family order be restored if we are to see a change in our world. When we begin to experience restoration and not just talk about it, we will see a change in the mindsets of our children and, in turn, in the morals, values and integrity of our world. It is important that we go back to old foundational family values. I believe that when family order is restored, we will see sons and daughters confident in who they are and what God has made them. Every positive change in the world begins with the foundation of family. Start changing the way in which we raise and discipline our children at home and you will see great results in our community.

Point

Family foundational values and principles are the start to a better world.

In a subtle way, we have rejected the true essence of motherhood and what it really means. We have become so busy pursuing our personal dreams and desires, that we become selfish and have neglected our natural roles of taking care of home. It's okay to pursue your dreams, but not to forsake your God-given ability to pour into your family. Don't be a smashing success at the expense of your family.

We have become selfish and no longer care about what really matters: our family. I honor God because in the midst of taking care of everyone else, I am blessed with a loving husband who gives me everything I could ever want, and children who love and adore me as their mother. We must live every day knowing that a day lost will not be returned. Make the best of each day.

When your children are young, try to live your life so that you won't have any regrets. As your children come of age, give them an example and a good moral base to build their future on. Each generation should be better than the former.

Overall, the marriage rate is declining. In spite of this, we need to stay true to God's design: men and women coming together, getting married, being fruitful (as the Bible says) and multiplying. While marriage rates go down, divorce rates rise at an alarming rate. We are definitely experiencing an age of non-commitment and low tolerance. People are less likely to work out their differences, and stay married. Instead they part ways due to their problems. Tolerance is at an all-time low with no regard to the repercussions of divorce and a broken-home. Society has less tolerance, patience, dedication and common sense than previous generations.

MODERN DAY MIX-UP

I understand that there are a lot of deadbeat dads who refuse to take responsibility for their families. Men who beat their wives and abandon their children. Yes, they do exist. But, on the flip side, there are also women who abuse their husbands and abandon their families as well. There are so many women who are the victim of assault in America. There are cases of abused women, abused men, and abused children. There are all sorts of other horrible behaviors that prove the "moral fabric of the family is in danger.

Let's be clear: all men are not dogs, nor does every woman disregard male authority. We need each other. As we understand the individual roles that God has created for us, we will respect and embrace that there are distinct differences between men and women.

Although there are distinct differences, we all are created equal by God to fulfill our purpose on earth.

The fact that two individuals are different does not mean that one is better than the other. We can appreciate those differences, even if we don't agree.

I am thankful that I have a loving husband, who is an awesome father to my children, and does not run away from the responsibility of providing for our family. A true man will be determined to provide for his family and will never be satisfied with struggle. I salute my husband, Don William Shelby Jr. It is easy to submit to and follow Don anywhere.

HOME SWEET HOME

Every home is different. Every situation is different. My advice is to seek God and find out what works best for your home. Whether you are married, single or a single parent, it is imperative that you set goals and strategies that will help you or your family thrive. Although we may look at excellent role models in families, it's important to know that what works in one family may not work in another.

Apply the word of God, and then embrace the love and concern that God exemplifies every day for your family. The key is to remain prayerful and work together to make your home one that is God fearing and where God can be glorified.

Teach your sons to honor "who" they are and "who" they will become: men of valor and respect. Pour into your sons and teach them attributes of a loving man of God, a good son, husband and father.

Fathers, I would like to share this: your sons emulate your behavior, and they are learning how to be a husband and father based on how you treat their mother, their sisters and them. More importantly, they watch how you handle conflict, business and everyday situations. Teach your sons truth, empathy and honesty. Teach them how to love and take responsibility for their actions.

Mothers, teach your daughters to be loving and virtuous and to exhibit the principles of truth, integrity, honesty and respect. I believe that the mother is a nurturer by natural instinct, if she embraces it. Most importantly, teach your daughters balance and to embrace their femininity. Again, your daughters will learn how to be a wife and mother, perhaps a professional career woman, by your example. Although they may view life through their own lens, you are definitely key in the adjustment and focus of that lens. You protect them and therefore your lifestyle and personality will have a great bearing on their outlook on life and in their behavior.

Connectedness to God and your family and everyday life will be key in forming your child(ren's) view of life.

Mothers, teach your daughters that *they can have it all.* Why Not?

Fathers, teach your sons to be strong and vigilant men.

Finally, parents: teach your children to be God-fearing citizens. Teach them to embrace their gender and God given identity. *Teach them that they can have it all! Why not?*

THE BUCK STOPS HERE!!

The power to break generational curses lies within your personal conviction. Personal decisions will determine your level of success and God will use you to repair and build a bridge from your generation to the next. You will be named the" repairer of the breach."

> And they that shall be of thee shall build the old waste places: thou shalt raise up the foundations of many generations; and thou shalt be called, The repairer of the breach, The restorer of paths to dwell in. (Isaiah 58:12 KJV)

A generational curse could be a traumatic situation that your parents or grandparents endured and which every generation after has felt the aftershocks of. God will speak to you of how to bring restoration into your life and break old cycles of poverty, no love, sexual addiction, depression, divorce, negative personality traits and so on. God will share with you and direct you to overcome every obstacle of your past that has hindered your breakthrough.

Take time now to pray and seek God for a specific strategy for your life, home and future. Then build your life upon a strong foundation of principles, morals and empathy.

Make a decision that whatever you lacked in your personal life or whatever the pains of the previous generation, you will no longer lack or be held hostage to the sins of your forefathers.

The generational curse will not repeat itself, but it will be broken. The buck stops here—with you!!!

ARE YOUR HANDS CLEAN?

Generational curses are real and so is "spiritual infection". I had a defining moment many years ago regarding the transfer of spirits from parents to children. Parents must realize that when they are blessed to watch over and raise their children that God is holding them accountable for their children's lives. When a child is young they are so impressionable.

I once received a revelation that when a mother has perverted or sinful ways and she does something as simple as change her baby's diaper or fix their food when her hands are dirty, she is transferring bad spirits as well as exposure to germs, disease and exemplifying poor behavior.

If you can catch a cold/flu, then it is possible to "catch and transfer a spirit."

I believe that your expectations for your child should be greater than they are for yourself, so you must therefore lead by example. You are held accountable for those impressionable years when everything a child has learned has been at your discretion. If you don't want your children to be perverts, then don't you be a pervert; if you don't want your child to consume alcohol or take drugs, then it's not rocket science: don't you drink alcohol or take drugs.

Start today by cleaning your hands and be cognoscente of your behavior. I am not painting a picture of parents as perfect people because we all make mistakes, but once you realize that a mistake has been made, correct it quickly so that it won't affect your seed (children). Clean your hands.

THE IMPORTANCE OF CONNECTING WITH A MENTOR

Earlier in the book I gave examples of great mentors. Now let's discuss the importance of connecting with a mentor. The purpose of a mentor is to guide you towards building a firmer foundation in your life. A Godly mentor, with Godly insight, is valuable as they can advise you on the important matters of life. A mentor or "life coach" may be called in for a specific project or goal that you desire to reach. There are important traits that I encourage everyone to look for when searching for a mentor.

TRAITS OF A GREAT MENTOR

1. They love God.
2. They are successful.
3. They have integrity and are honest.
4. They are pure of heart.
5. They have succeeded where you hope to succeed.
6. They genuinely want you to succeed.
7. They love you and everything that is connected to you.

For example, if you are married, it is important that they (your mentor) at least like your spouse. If you have children, they should appreciate and want to see the best in your children. I use the word "like" and "appreciate" because, say you have an abusive spouse, they may not agree with your spouse's behavior towards you. If your friend helps to guide and support you in your troubles, and if you desire to stay married, it is critical that they maintain a clear and *unbiased* focus on what you desire, not what they may think is best for you. They must have a heart for your spouse and be concerned for the wellbeing of your family, all while standing for truth. Make sure that your mentor is trustworthy.

YOUR RELATIONSHIP WITH GOD

Even the greatest mentor can't give you every element of your individual plan. Why? Because they are not you. You have to receive your master plan directly from God. What is God saying to you? What is your personal conviction?

The only way you will find out is to listen and develop an intimate personal relationship with God. He has a plan specific to you and your mission here on earth. Pray today and get your blueprint from the throne room of God. Then put it into practice.

It's important to realize that you won't be perfect and do everything right all the time. You may veer off the path, but that doesn't mean you give up on "His" plan for your life. Remember that God has not changed his mind about loving you and your family. It is His extended grace that holds the door open, and it is God that gives you the power to get back on track. Make a decision to commit to the process of your development, spiritually and naturally.

As believers we can have it all! You don't have to sacrifice one thing for another. The Bible says we should prosper even as our souls prosper. In other words, we should pray for the ability to multi-task and everything that we accomplish should be better because of the anointing that we have on our lives.

You can commit to God, get your education, and still have the anointing to fulfill God's plan for your life. As we take responsibility and submit to God's plan, we will begin to see change in the moral fabric of society, because we understand *whom*, as well as *whose*, we are. Remain committed and connected to God and the sky no longer becomes the limit. With commitment and confidence, you can reach further than you have ever dreamed. Why Not Have It All!

A MOTHER'S LOVE

No one can replace the love of a mother or the gentle touch of a wife. To be honest, as a mother, I don't think we want anyone to replace who we are (or should be) in our husband's or our children's lives.

It's no secret: more women are in the workforce than ever before, and we have the right to pursue professions just as much as men. But, a well-balanced woman can do it all. If they choose to be in the workforce, they must know how to skillfully *balance* work and home. There is a positional anointing that comes with being a mother and wife. We can leap over walls and conquer anything that is going on in our career, family or with our children.

Again, let's be clear: a working woman shouldn't feel bad about her decision to work and pursue her professional dream. They should seek God to find out the plan that works best for their situation. God can and will give them the grace to succeed in the workplace and in the home. I might add, never ever let the things of God go lacking. Everything starts with the foundation of a God fearing relationship and your service to God and His house.

MY STORY, PART EIGHT

My mom is a great educator and the mother of five children. She attended city council meetings every week to secure funding for her day care center and she worked eight hours a day. Every Thursday my mom would pick me up (after she got off work) and off we went to the City Council Meetings. She would give me a legal pad and pen, sit me in the chair beside her and give instructions. She would show me the agenda and where her business appeared on it. Then she would ask that I take thorough notes so that she could review them in case she missed anything.

To date I am one of the greatest note takers ever! I gained that knowledge because of a mother that took time to not only teach me but take me along for the ride. Note: she didn't leave me at home, neither drop me off at the sitter, she found a way to "baby-sit" me at the council meeting. She found a creative (wise) way to spend quality time and teach a life lesson on taking notes and how to conduct a business meeting.

Every morning, she would get up and fix breakfast before I went to school. She would pack lunches, and played a major role in my education. She washed and ironed all of the clothes (my dad never had to iron a shirt) and she fixed his lunch every night as he worked nights. She literally did it all.

My parents stayed in constant communication with my teachers and my mom was active at my school. My teachers, as well as my principal, knew my parents because of their concern when it came to my education.

I remember when I started 6th grade and the school district that we lived in was not the best. Because my Mother was an educator, she met with the school superintendent and requested that I be allowed to enroll in a predominately white school because they were sound academically in state testing etc... The school board granted my mother's request after months of going back and forth. She also asked that they provide transportation, along with one other black student to the new school. Again, her request was honored.

I can remember the many challenges of being a black student in an "all-white" school. Integration was not prominent at the time. As a matter of fact, my transfer was one of the first for the city of Ypsilanti who at that time was comprised of a predominately black student population on the south side of town and predominately white students on the other. Every day, I went through the first month of going into the lunchroom and as soon as I walked in, the white students would begin to beat on the table and start chanting, "Black, Black, Black.! After they erupted into the chant afterwards they would laugh uncontrollably. The first time it happened, I was stunned because, I didn't know this type of racism or behavior existed. I was taught to love *all* people and not to make a difference because of the color of a person's skin. I cried every day. My mother who never reacted quickly because she wanted all of her children to learn how to handle conflict, listened to my complaint. She instructed me to ignore them at first but after coming home every day with the same complaint and the teachers and principal who were in the lunchroom did absolutely nothing, my mother said, its time to respond. I'll never forget that day, my mom got up that morning did her normal routine and on my way to the bus, she told me to expect a visit to my school around lunch time. As promised, she showed up at 11:30 went into the Principals office and demanded an explanation. I felt relieved to know that *today*...I had back-up: Mom was in the building! The bell rang and I walked down to the lunchroom. I think everybody knew something was up this day, because when I walked in everybody looked and said nothing at all. I believe they received a warning that my Mom was on her way. My Mom walked in with my principal waved at me across the room and stood in the middle of the lunchroom and asked everyone to quiet themselves because she had something to say. She said, "I am Bonita's Mom" She said, "Bonita has made me aware that she is experiencing something that I am not too happy with." "Bonita is African American and a young lady with a bright future, she is not black". "I want to know who in this room is beating on tables and calling her "black" when she walks in the lunchroom?" I left my job because I felt the need to address the student or students that continue to display this type of behavior." "I encourage you to stop and this will be the last time that I will have to leave my job teaching students just as yourself to address this issue". "If Bonita comes home another day and tells me that she is having this problem, I will come and see you (she was talking to the principal) and I will have to invite her father as well as the Superintendent of schools to address this problem, do you all understand?' All of the students felt the Mama's "I ain't playing with y'all" voice and they said, "Yes ma'am, we are sorry". Well I never had another issue from that day. As a matter of fact I had more friends than I could handle. My Mom is still my hero, at home and in the workplace. She did it ALL!

My mother would prepare dinner each day, she took care of the house (which was and still is always spick and span). Mom would take care of me and my siblings and to this day she says that her children are her pride and joy. She is a great example of what a "woman" and "mother" can do under the anointing of being a "God fearing wife" and mother. Although she worked every day, dinner was always on the table.

On Saturdays, without fail, we would wake up early, and spend family time, starting with breakfast. After breakfast we would have plans to shop and then go out for lunch. We never missed a Saturday together. My mother is my 'Shero'. To me, she is a super wonder woman" personified.

Sunday's all day was dedicated to church services day and night. (At times all day.)

Mom's example of balance, from a very young age, shaped who I desired to become and established my belief that it could be done. I knew that I would pursue my education because of what she had accomplished. I knew I would be a business woman, because she had invested in teaching me about business. Most importantly, I saw a God fearing, successful mother whom I knew would impact not only my life but many generations' to come.

I saw her in action, and now that I am a wife and the mother of five, I understand the conscious effort it took to run our house. I knew that I could make it happen because of the example my mom set before me.

I know that I can do *anything* in my life as long as I keep God first. *Why not have it all!* That is Gods desire and will for your life. You can have **balance**, experience great success .and be happy!

MY STORY, PART NINE NO REGRETS

When Don and I were first married, we were in a horrible car accident. The fact that I am writing this proves that God protected us from what could have been a tragedy.

Don and I were told that we would not be able to have children. But that's not what God said.

When we found out that we were expecting our first child I was so excited and promised God that every child He gave to us, I would in turn give back to Him (God). When it was all said and done, God gave us five (the biblical number for grace) beautiful children.

After I had my third child, my loving husband talked with me about the care of our children and he asked how I was feeling. Of course, I shared how hard it was to leave the children and go to work. I was working a full time job at the hospital, I was in college, I was taking care of my home, and I was (I am) a Pastor's wife. Don immediately gave me the option to stay home with the children and continue my college education. He shared that he would take the steps necessary to make sure that our family was taken care of, so Don worked three jobs.

He held down a marketing job, worked at the bank during the day, and at a fast food restaurant at night. I can remember going to my room and crying, overwhelmed by the sincere desire to help my husband. I wanted to contribute something to the household, but couldn't --financially. As I look back… I *did* invest in the care of my family-- something that is priceless and cherished. Something in which I have no regrets.

It was so sweet of my husband to move to Ypsilanti so I could finish my college education. This spoke volumes about his love for me. We lived in married housing for two years until Don III was born and, looking back, God supplied us with what we needed and every circumstance worked for our good.

As a young wife and mother, I had dreams and aspirations and I knew that I would make a difference in this world. I just had to find that balance. To date, I am still striving for better ways to balance my life and be successful.

Don and I never wanted to look back once our children had become adults and have regrets of not giving our children everything they needed to live a successful, God fearing life. I always said that when my children grew up, I wouldn't be that parent loaded with guilt and regrets about how they had been raised. I took time out, and made great sacrifices to invest in my children. My mandate was to find balance in my home and pursue my personal goals and dreams.

It was not always easy; children do not come with an instruction manual, but God taught me to be a good wife, loving mother, Bishop's wife and more.

Was I perfect at everything?

No, but I got my plan from the Father, stayed in prayer, and I have the support of a loving husband and it is continually working out. Although (when my children were young), I felt that I gave my all as I look back in retrospect, maybe I could have done more. No matter what you accomplish, if given the opportunity to go back and do some things over again …we would.

Stay committed, stay connected and loyal to the plan of God and everything will work out fine.

10 THE UNLOVABLES

Are you "unlovable"? We have to be careful that we don't become individuals who are in a constant war with ourselves.

'Unlovables' build walls. They feel like they are the victim and that everyone is against them (including God). Do not make yourself unlovable; open up and allow God to heal you of the past hurts, rejection and pain so that you can experience the love of the Father and others.

Make a decision to enjoy this beautiful world and embrace love. God has so much more that He wants to share with you.

As a Pastor's wife, I had to realize through much trial and error that some people have different capacities for love, and they can only love at the capacity in which they are capable. Dependent upon their upbringing and past rejections, they may not show love at all, nor open themselves up to be loved. Yet they have so much love to give.

When dealing with an unlovable, I would find myself getting frustrated at times because it seemed like the more love I gave, the more I was rejected. After taking time out to counsel and getting to know and understand the individual, I discovered that it wasn't me at all. It was their own personal limitations, caused by past pain, which caused them to shut me out. Many women are single because they are "unloveable"., In other words because of past hurt rejection or simply being stuck in their ways, they don't know how to "love" nor recognize true love. When they can open up, get rid of the hurt and stop being irritated and frustrated, that's when God will reveal their "mate."

As a Pastor's wife, I have had many direct experiences with unloveables. Once, in a moment of ministry, I had to give stern instruction to a young woman who had a tumultuous relationship with her biological mother. She immediately shut down, experiencing the same feelings she did as a child when receiving her mom's punishment and verbal abuse, because my tone brought back bad memories. Through years of constantly feeling the pain of rejection, she had become distant with her mom. She couldn't understand why she deserved such misery. It was my position and place to build trust and let her know that I loved her regardless of how she treated me.

Whenever you deal with an *unlovable,* try to understand that there is always a cause for their behavior. When you take the time to get to know them and get to the root of their behavior, you will find a loving person who really wants to open up but often can't muster enough strength to trust and move beyond those past feelings of rejection. If you want to help an *unlovable* move beyond isolation and hurt, you should remain consistent in their life and constantly show love and support. It is important to pray for them, and patiently wait, because after they are convinced that you are genuine, they will gain the trust to open up and experience love without barriers.

LOVE IS A "STRONG" WORD

A former member of our congregation never received hugs, nor heard the words "I love you," as a child. They came to church every Sunday and our staff would greet them at the door with "I love you". When I saw them, I always gave them a hug and an "I love you". They thought that hugs and love were false, like a joke. They would cringe every time a hug was given or the word 'love' was used.

With hugs every Sunday and God revealing my *true* and *real heart,* the individual began to trust again, and I saw the fortified walls that they had built up through the years...come down.

Now, they are one of the biggest *huggers* in the church! They find me every Sunday with a smile and say, "I love you so much." In turn, they are now spreading that love to others. That's a success story.

Meet people where they are and allow them to grow into the love you exemplify—with a pure heart and no motives or strings attached. Understand that if they never embrace hugging, then even a handshake and constant stability in your personality will help more than you could imagine. Constant and abiding love breaks down barriers.

As a mother, make it a point to tell your husband, children or loved one that you love them every day.

11 THE LIONESS AND HER CUBS

Lions are known to be fearless and strong. Revered as the *king* and *queen* of the jungle, when challenged or threatened, they are a force to be reckoned with. Not only are lions fierce, they have beauty, courage and boldness that speak to their strength and honor.

Even more legendary than their dominant nature is the way in which a lioness protects her cubs from harm and danger. Her care extends beyond her pride or group. The lioness will not only take care of her own, but she will instinctively take care of other neglected cubs that are not theirs. Her responsibility is to give those whom she cares for a chance to survive in a jungle where predators await the opportunity to devour them.

The lioness will not only teach her cubs how to survive in the wild, but she will also defend and protect what is hers. In turn, she rears a *fearless* lion. The lioness invests in teaching survival and courage to raise new *kings* and *queens* of the jungle. The lioness is aware of every necessity to preparing them for the future. While the male lion is the clear leader of the pride, the female protects the family, forming the next generation of leaders.

BACK IN THE DAY

In generations past, neighbors would nurture and discipline every child in the neighborhood. There was a certain bond that mothers had not only with their children, but with every child.

The mothers of old sincerely wanted every child to do well and this is what separates "modern day" motherhood from times past.

THE SIGNIFICANCE OF A SPIRITUAL MOTHER

The instinctive nature of a lioness can be paralleled in so many ways to the role of a mother or spiritual mother. There is great significance in how a lioness cares not only for her own but for others as well. A spiritual mother works hard to restore anything that a person may have lacked in their life. Her major concern is the spiritual and natural wellbeing of all spiritual sons and daughters. You don't have to give birth to someone to love them as your very own.

As Mothers, we have the responsibility to teach survival and raise fearless children of God. We must equip this generation with the "know-how" to sustain themselves in the jungle of life. It is a jungle out there, and only the strong will thrive.

A FAMILY, NOT BY ACCIDENT

Don proposed to me five years after we began dating. I immediately accepted, knowing he was God's perfect choice for me. We are still so much in love. Upon acceptance of Don's proposal, we started planning the wedding; ordering dresses and tuxes, saving the date, choosing invitations, etc., etc.

All I could think about was, "Wow, we are finally going to get married."

"Don and Bonita Shelby." I loved saying that to myself!

In the middle of planning the wedding, Don was scheduled to go back to college at Tennessee State University, where he would complete his senior year, and then enroll in law school.

With one day left in Michigan, Don wanted to spend some time, so we decided (along-with my sister) to attend a concert in Detroit. We loved spending time together whenever we could, because he lived so far away and would be attending college even further away.

On Saturday afternoon, Don drove down and picked my sister and I up. We headed off to the concert and had a great time. While the event was memorable, what happened on the way home would completely change our lives forever.

After the concert ended, Don decided to take the back roads home as opposed to the highway. We were traveling down Michigan Avenue, talking, when "it" happened.

A drunk driver came from out of nowhere, on the wrong side of the road, and hit us head on at 85 mph.

The only thing that I can remember is a loud crash and then a sizzling sound. I awoke to the screams of my sister and groans of pain and agony. When I came to, my face was in the passenger's seat and I was *butt first* headed out of a cracked windshield. I managed to wiggle my body and turn around. I looked over at Don and his face was bloody and he was unconscious. The steering wheel had bent up and hit Donny in the mouth. I peeked into the back seat and there was my sister, screaming, with large, jagged pieces of glass sticking out of her head. The windshield had shattered and flown backwards.

I felt as if I was in a nightmare. I then blacked out. When I awoke, scared, I began to call on Jesus. All of a sudden, the drunk driver came to my window and said, "Why are you calling on Jesus? He can't help you, you are going to die out here!"

At that moment I understood the plans of the enemy and that was to kill all of us, so I grabbed hold of my strength and begin to scream the name of *Jesus* louder. I screamed so hard that I blacked out again. This time when I came to I was standing outside of the car. I know it was an angel of the Lord that lifted me out of the car that day. As I came to my senses, I saw that my sister Marvetta had also got out of the car and, because of the trauma to her face, was running frantically (in shock) down the road in heels.

I had on a black dress and heels. My arm felt numb and I could only use my left hand. The road was pitch black and the driver of the car that hit us had run off into the woods. The accident was now classified a "hit and run".

The road was dark. I looked at the car stretched across the road and realized that Don was still trapped inside. I ran to his side of the car and stood watch so that I could wave and scream for help. About ten minutes later a car came down the road at 60 miles per hour and couldn't see the car (or me) because it was dark and I was in all black. The car was about two feet away when they realized that we were on the road. The car spun out of control and ran onto the grass. I didn't move from the car, because I wanted to protect Donny from being struck again. I can remember seeing the headlights swerving and I can hear the screeching sound of the cars spinning out of control.

Three cars in total did the exact same, and I knew then that satan was out to destroy us. There were four attempts on our lives that night, but to God's glory we survived to tell the story.

The impact was so great that Don was trapped in the car and had to be cut out with a saw and lifted out.

As I stated earlier, Don and I were engaged to be married, and we were in the middle of planning a wedding for the following May. The wedding was the least of our worries at the time; we were more concerned about the news that we had just received from the doctor. Don was told that, because of the severity of his injuries, he would never walk again. His leg had been severed—sliced in half—by the dashboard, and was hanging on by a string of flesh.

After 6 weeks in the hospital, Don returned home.

After 3 weeks of getting accustomed to using a wheelchair, he called to let me know that he understood if I wanted to call off the wedding. He went on to explain that he felt that he would not be able to fulfill his responsibility of being a husband considering the prognosis that he would never walk again.

I knew that I totally and absolutely loved Don and wanted to spend the rest of my life with this amazing man. I told Donny that I would not cancel the wedding, and that we would believe that God would let him walk again. Don went to physical therapy four times a week and had to be assisted in the simplest things, such as being carried to the bathroom, bathed etc.

I picked up the phone one evening to let Don know how much I loved him and how excited I was to spend the rest of my life with him. He responded, "I can't be everything to you that I desire, I love you enough to let you go and my desire is that you to move on with your life and find someone else."

My response was, "Donny, I love you with my whole heart and if I have to push you in a wheelchair for the rest of my life, I will. If you were burned and unrecognizable, I would still love and marry you!"

Don got quiet and said, "Well you pray for me, but I still desire that you move on with your life."

Of course, I told him, "No".

Teary-eyed and sad, I took a giant leap of faith and told Don that I would continue planning the wedding and on May 9th, I would be standing at the altar to marry him. I also told him that he had better show up and not leave me hanging!

As months passed, one day in physical therapy God gave Don a word of healing to try and walk. He mustered up enough strength to take the first step which was a bit wobbly, got back up tried again and has been walking/running ever since.

On that glorious day of May 9th, God gave us a supernatural miracle and Don came walking down the aisle with an audience of 700 well-wishers in attendance and met me at the altar. Having spent a year of his life in a wheelchair, our wedding day was indeed a "celebration of love".

God is faithful, and my love story was just beginning and to date I still thank God for placing this special man in my life. Don is a living, walking and breathing miracle. He is a testament of God's supernatural healing power, and we will never forget God's mercy and goodness.

THE HONEYMOON IS OVER

The week after our honeymoon, Don officially moved to Ypsilanti so that I could pursue my college education. We were approved and excited to get our first apartment in married housing. We both registered for classes and were full-time, working students.

One month later, I went to the doctor for a routine checkup and he told me something that would rock my world. The doctor said that, because of injuries sustained from the accident and the trauma to my pelvis, I would never be able to bear children. Of course, I was absolutely devastated. My hubby and I were just beginning our marriage and we get this news?

I came home, cried uncontrollably, and fell into Don's arms. He kissed me and looked me in the eye and said, "God is in control, and we will have children."

During the next three months we prayed fervently and petitioned God with all of our hearts. We promised God that if He gave us children (Don originally wanted ten!), we would give all of them back to him. We promised to teach our children moral goodness and raise an army that would advance the Kingdom of God. To date, the Shelby crew is doing just that!

Even though the doctor said one thing, we believed that God was greater. We prayed, and would constantly buy pregnancy tests only to be disappointed. We would pray and buy tests until one day (eleven months later), I came home and the test showed that God had answered our prayers: I was pregnant!

> **Point**
>
> Doctors may say one thing, but God has the final say!

Now, we have five beautifully talented (adult) children that are my blessing and a testament to the power of God. The Shelby 5! God gave me grace and favor, and I'm thankful! This is why I am adamant about giving my children my all, because God gave me precious gifts. I made a vow to love my children unconditionally and teach them to reverence and honor God with their lives. I kept my promise to God because He in turn kept His promise to me.

FAMILY IS EVERYTHING

Our family Motto over the past six years has been "Family is everything."

I take the privilege of being a mother very seriously because God entrusted innocent lives into my hands. As mothers we have a tremendous responsibility: to nurture and teach our children (to the best of our ability) by example.

I always say that when children are born they are like little sponges that soak up information, and it does not make a difference if that information is good or bad—they will absorb it. In our human frailty, we must strive each day to be on our best behavior, so that our children and all those we come into contact with can see goodness exemplified.

Just like the lioness, we are not only committed to our own children, but we can speak to and impact the lives of neglected children as well. Whether you have naturally birthed children or not, as a woman you are qualified to nurture others. Men are qualified to teach and nurture as well. We tend to think that we have to be a certain age to mentor or nurture others, but God can use any woman (any age) that is obedient and has something positive to give. God is in need of men and women that will accept the challenge to touch as many lives as they can.

I can remember the voice of God sharing guidance as to how I should raise my children and the type of mother that He (God) requires. My husband and I had many meaningful conversations before our first child was born. We discussed how we would discipline, raise, and nurture our children.

Don III, our firstborn, was two years old when my husband accepted the call to become a Pastor and start a ministry. We went back to the drawing board, because we knew that this was an added dimension to our parenthood.

Now that my husband was called to pastor, not only would we be responsible for our children, but now my husband and I would carry the responsibility of the development and nurturing of spiritual sons and daughters as well. That's another book altogether (and it's coming soon).

My husband and I understood the commitment that it would take to be good parents, to grow a healthy church, affect lives, and build our ministry.

At the time, I was working a full-time job, and I prayed for a strategy to *balance* my life. I also sought God's direction as to how to raise God fearing and happy children. My husband and I decided that while maintaining our ministry, we wanted clear rules about what we *would* and *would not* do when it came to raising our children.

DECLARATION

Don and I made a declaration to:

- Teach our children about God by example

- Never gossip in our children's presence (neither outside of their presence)

- Teach them to see the good in all people, but raise them to recognize that there are some bad people, though "bad" people can change.

- Raise them not to see color or race, but to see everyone as a child of God

- Spend quality time with our children, collectively and individually

- Have family discussions consistently

- Give back to the less fortunate

- Have a heart for the sick and disabled

- Take care of each other, our children and our home

- Maintain our roles and personal responsibilities: I as their mother would quit my job to be their nurturer; Don would stabilize the ministry. I would stay close to Dons side

- Allow our children to develop their own characters, and be comfortable in their own skin

- Allow our children to be free and enjoy life, and not raise them in a box

- Live by our family motto: "Do good and good will follow you."

- Teach them the importance of family

- Dispel the negative title of "preacher's kids". They are not obnoxious brats!

- Don and I made a choice not to accept negativity or bad advice from bitter, frustrated parents

- Teach them to love people with the Love of God, and to understand that hurting people hurt people

- Teach them the importance of education

- Teach them the importance of honesty and integrity through teachable moments and life lessons

- Keep them clean and well dressed—your children are a reflection of you

- Teach social graces and etiquette

- Tell our Children that we love them as well as tell each other.

- Discipline them with love- never prove a point to others by degrading or devaluing our children

- Stay of one accord as their parents and never allow our children to "put two ends against the middle."

A MOTHER'S PRAYER

Pray and ask God to give you instruction as to how to raise your children. If you are the mother of more than one, ask God for collective and individual instruction.

EXERCISE

Write a prayer for your children here

_____

_____

_____

_____

_____

_____

_____

_____

_____

_____

_____

_____

_____

_____

_____

_____

_____

_____

_____

_____

_____

_____

_____

SAY THIS PRAYER

Father,

I am a protector and a nurturer. It is my duty to raise my children in the fear and admonition of God. My promise from the word of God is that if I train my child in the way they should go, when they are old, they will not depart from it. There may be times when one of my children may depart from your teaching, God, but just like the prodigal son, my prayer is that you let them find their way back home.

I pray for strength and direction, and that I would be a mother after your own heart, O God. Lead, guide and direct me in all truth. Allow your grace and mercy to follow me and my child(ren), for all the days of our lives. Give me strength to stand on every word that you declare over my child's life, even when they were in my womb. Give knowledge and wisdom of how to execute that plan and not waver.

I understand that my role in my child's life is to provide stability, constant faith and abiding love.

Amen

NOBODY'S PERFECT

Realize that your children may not be perfect, but neither are you... nor anyone else. Know that with God's help, we can give them a strong (resilient) foundation to stand on for the rest of their lives. We can guide and raise them with truth and understanding of God's word and their destiny. After we commit to raising them with love for God, honesty and integrity, we can then place everything that concerns them into God's hands.

CELEBRATE MILESTONES

It is important that we celebrate our children's accomplishments. Many times, we focus solely on our children's pitfalls and mistakes. Early on, I realized that if I wanted my children to succeed and live "purpose driven" lives, I would have to celebrate not one milestone, but many. It started with birthdays and positive reinforcement. I took every good deed and every honorable act as a milestone. Milestones build character, and with each milestone came an appreciation and their subsequent desire for the next step.

I have always deemed birthdays something special. Each year that God gives life to my children, is a celebration. I have hosted so many parties that were perfectly planned from princess in "pink parties" to parties on the farm, from skating to pizza and bowling, etc. Every year there was a theme and much strategic planning, so that my children would know just how special they are to their dad and I. Good Christian parties at our house have always been a *"big deal"*.

Other celebrated accomplishments included graduations (at every level, from kindergarten to college). Each year the celebration would be a little bigger. We held dinners after graduation ceremonies, and my husband and I would share (along with family and friends) how proud we were of our child(ren), on that particular milestone, and encourage each as they moved to the next level (step).

Back in the day, parents only deemed high school and college graduation as moments to celebrate. But modern day parents are learning to celebrate every step of the way. In my opinion, this builds confidence and ambition. It also allows your child to feel a sense of accomplishment as their parents. Parents arise! Take notice and celebrate *every* positive step.

We are our Father's children, and God is cheering us on every day to *be* and *do* our absolute best.

I believe that the more positive reinforcements you give as a parent; the more positive results you will see. Make a point to protect your children and pour love into their lives. Recognize their good/bad traits and let your child know that you are proud of their successes and that your love is unconditional. When or if mistakes happen, or they don't hit the target every time, they will have a positive memory of your feedback as well as remembering your expectations, and then they will know that you love them regardless. In turn they will strive for perfection even if they don't hit the target. I call this new trend, "love to greatness. "In good and bad, let them know that one factor remains your love, hope and expectation, let them know although disappointed (at times), you won't give up on them. This is the representation of true love and family...resilience.

My husband and I have dedicated an entire room in our home entitled, "The Shelby Wall of Fame." Every wall is covered from ceiling to floor with awards, certificates, and newspaper articles from kindergarten to college on all five children. Academic honors are on the top of the list and trophies line the shelf. Our children reflect on their accomplishments and know how proud we are when they step in the room. It becomes a constant reminder of their success.

It is important that you make your requests/expectations known and let your children know just how proud you are to call them yours. Let them know that not only are you counting on them, God is counting on them to make a difference in the lives of others in this world.

TEACHABLE MOMENTS

As we raise children, we have chances to use everyday occurrences to teach them what *to do* and what *not to do*.

I remember a time when one of my children accidentally picked up a pack of gum at the store when they were very young. I didn't realize that we hadn't paid for the item until I got back to the car.

With all five of my babies, some still in the cart, and some holding my hand, I started belting them in and unloading bags. I saw in the clutches of the last baby a pack of bubblegum, and a little sinister smile on their face as if to say, "Look what I found! And it's all mine…"

I used this as a teachable moment for the baby and for all of my children. I told them, "You never take anything that you do not pay for—that's called stealing. I know it was a mistake, but never let that happen again."

I wanted them to know that if they needed anything, they should ask. I spoke with them about the consequences of stealing. I also expressed that in their lifetime, I never wanted them to desire something so badly that they would steal to get it. I taught them the principles of hard work: whatever they want or need in life, with hard work and good stewardship, they can obtain. I shared that we might not always have exactly what we want, but God supplies everything we need.

After I addressed the issue, I unpacked all five children, went back into the store and took the gum back. It is important that you allow your children to see an example of integrity and honesty in your actions. This rule of our house was reinforced from that day forward. The sales clerk couldn't believe that I had unpacked all five of my children and walked back into the store to return a pack of gum.

It is important that you allow your children to see integrity and honesty in action. They are watching and it is through observation that life's most valuable lessons are learned. Don't have the mentality, "Do as I say, but don't do as I do." That is living a hypocritical lifestyle and can eventually make you a stumbling block. A child's formative years are with you and you are shaping their future morals, for the most part by your actions.

Have you ever wondered why so many children rebel when they grow older and run away from the church feeling like everything that appears right seems phony? Could it be that you have lived a lie at home and all they witnessed was a hypocritical lifestyle?

I know as parents we are not at all perfect, but for the sake of your children and even the people that you influence, give trying to live right your best shot!

ONE BIG HAPPY FAMILY

I never expected anyone else to raise and care for my children. I can honestly say that I took my children everywhere that I went. There were only a few people I would trust to babysit them and when you saw one of us, you saw all of us, as a family. The tribe of Shelby, seven strong!

Times when my husband and I had to go away, I would write a twenty-seven-page manual with day-to-day operations of how I desired them to be cared for. "The Shelby Manual" would contain everything the trusted caregiver would need to know about my children; temperaments, meal planning, daily schedules, emergency contact information, medical releases, etc. My husband and I would leave money so that keeping our children wouldn't be a financial burden nor boring. Planned activities were a part of the babysitting plan, such as movies, shopping, pizza parties, etc.

I would iron all of their clothes before leaving home. Each child's clothes would not only be in their drawer, but I went as far as to get labeled bins with each of their clothes, undergarments etc. to make things easily accessible to the sitter. Each hand-selected babysitter was required to read and know the Shelby Manual before taking care of my children.

Now that I look back, I realize that I would wear myself out physically before going out of town. I remember getting on the plane, throwing my head back and crying because I had to leave my family. My husband would always help me realize that I needed a break and that it was okay. And it was okay, because, I was with my hubby . . . my best friend in the entire world.

When we were out, people would come up to me and admire how well behaved the children were; they weren't running out of control. I could take them anywhere and never worry about one of them lying on the floor, throwing a temper tantrum. I am thankful that a lot of our "parental promises" have been fulfilled, but there are more to come. Recently I had a trip with hubby and although they are grown I found myself washing everything in sight. I quickly came to my senses and went to bed. The heart to care never goes away!

MAKE THE INVESTMENT

My husband and I have invested in our children, talking with them, listening to them, praying over them and allowing God to direct them. Not only have we invested in them, we have tried hard to live the life we desire them to live. We know God has a perfect plan for each of them individually and collectively. Our desire (as parents) should be to challenge our children to achieve greatness.

A good steward is the mother that goes to God and in turn receives a plan of how to raise, invest and support her child(ren). After the parent receives the plan, they should pray and guide their children to the best of their ability. Again, children are not born with instruction manuals, but God has given every mother the instinct to nurture, protect and care for them.

The lioness protects her cub at all costs. She lets them venture out, within her sight, to try new things, but she always stands in close proximity, ready to pounce into action whenever the need arises.

Rise up, lioness, and become the mother God has intended. Remain fearless!

CHILDREN'S PRAYER

Here is a Prayer that I have prayed for our children:

Father,

I thank you for each gift that you have blessed to come forth through my womb. The seed that you have established and brought forth in our lives will in turn change lives and be great on the earth. Strengthen me to be the mother that you have ordained in the heavens. Grant me the boldness to execute your plan for my children and be ready to guard and protect what you have placed under my care. Give me that same love and compassion for others, and give me a heart for the growth and nourishment of children and people everywhere. I cherish motherhood and I embrace it.

Grant me wisdom and knowledge to be an example to my children and lead and guide them in righteousness. Anoint my hands as I care for them and keep my hands and my heart **pure.** Let them see the love of God exemplified in my life. Allow my children to see the love of a woman towards her husband and help me to honor and love my children's father with a pure and untainted love. Protect my heart and my mind and allow me to grow with my children and mature each day. Never allow pride to overtake any of us, but keep us with a forgiving heart and the ability to say, "I'm sorry" when necessary. Lord allow me to live life with "no regrets', teach me your way and guard me from pitfalls and detriment.

Keep my family in the center of your will and never let us go.

In Jesus' name,

Amen.

12 DON'T DRINK THE POISON

Life is too short to hold grudges and live your life seeking *payback*. This chapter will encourage you to forgive *everyone* and *everything* that has hurt you in your *past* and into your *present*. When you hold resentment in your heart, it's like being chained to your past and weighed down by it.

We all know someone who has held grudges and anger in their hearts to the point that they become sick, bitter and stressed by it. They live guarded lives and it is almost as if they are trapped in a dark dungeon in which nothing comes *in* and nothing goes *out*. Refusing to forgive a person for their actions means that you hold onto the stress those actions caused, and stress is often directly related to anxiety, medical problems and sickness.

Make a decision not to drink the "poison" of bitterness, jealousy, and hatred.

DON'T BE JEALOUS

> The Bible says, "jealousy is cruel as the grave."(Song of Solomon 8:6 KJV)

Point

Jealousy can break you financially or "bankrupt" you spiritually. Jealousy will keep you in poverty.

Jealousy can lead to obsession. Coveting is the desire (in an extreme manner) to have what someone else has. You covet when you feel as if the owner of the thing you want shouldn't be blessed with it, and you begin to compare their success with your success to the point that it becomes a stressful and unhealthy obsession.

There is absolutely no reason why you should be jealous of anyone. You were born to succeed, and you are fearfully and wonderfully made. Take your measure and work with it and get what you want for yourself!

Forgiveness is how Jesus responded after He endured the hardships inflicted on Him by those whom He fed, healed and delivered. Jesus asked His father to "forgive them; for they know not what they do." (Luke 23:34 KJV) Even 'til His death on the cross, His life exemplified *forgiveness*. We were guilty and Jesus still showed only mercy and grace.

This is the ultimate example of forgiveness, and with this, our perfect example, we must learn to forgive others and move on with life. I know that some of you have dealt with betrayal, molestation, rape, ridicule and much more, but for your own sake, free yourself today. Open yourself up to your bright future, and no longer be held hostage by self-inflicted pain that you carry because of anger and resentment. Make a choice to forgive and move on to pursuing your future dreams.

As you begin to forgive, you will experience an inner peace that only God can give. You are not responsible nor held accountable for the actions of others, but your actions only. Remember: the enemy wants you to live life bound by other people.

THE POISON OF BONDAGE

When you value other opinions of yourself more than you value your own, you are *bound*.

There was a time in my life when I would be consumed with how people felt concerning my decisions/actions. I would put too much emphasis on what other people thought of me. One day my dear husband (my Bishop) made a statement that was life changing: "Who cares what they think, you will never have to see them again anyway."

That day I was liberated to live my life, be free and make myself happy. We can't live our lives in constant fear of what other people think about our choices. We also can't spend valuable time holding onto resentment.

Certainly I'm not licensing anyone to be obnoxious and rude to anyone else, but we must develop the mentality that if we please God then we should feel *inner* peace. No longer live under a dark cloud of fear. You are what God has made you, and if others don't appreciate who you are, well… move on, say "Adios amigos!"

It's time to pronounce a benediction over those who don't appreciate your worth; say goodbye to people who really don't want to invest time in getting to know you, but judge you anyway. In the big scheme of things, they are only cheating themselves.

Recognize who you truly live for: God.

Know what your purpose is in life. You have a bright future, and once you release yourself from hurt, guilt and the people who inspire those feelings, you will find that you can turn your *pain* into *purpose*. Your life is a testimony that will help others. Take time, extend grace and forgive. If you carry the guilt of your past, know that you are forgiven. Move forward into brighter days and toward the fulfillment of your dream.

PRAYER OF FREEDOM

Father,

I thank you for my life, and today I ask that you forgive me even as I forgive others. Today, I choose to forgive and I release resentment from my will and heart. Those who have wronged me, hurt and discredited my self-worth, I forgive.

I thank you for my freedom and today I cut the cord of holding myself hostage to the evil actions of others. I know that healing of my body and mind is attached to forgiveness. I realize that the moment I free myself from the chains of anger, God will open up the heavens and give me peace.

My wealth is connected to my freedom. Give me the strength that I need to see everyone as you see them. Father, forgive me and forgive others from evil and destroy every root of jealousy, bitterness and strife. Help me to embrace my assignment and my self-worth.

Cleanse my heart and purify my mind. I extend grace and mercy to everyone that has hurt or betrayed me. Father, I forgive myself from my past. Lord, free me from all soul ties, and break every generational curse from my life. The curse stops here and I am free. I will not live chained to the guilt of my past mistakes, but I embrace my promising future.

Father, let me see others through the eyes of grace and mercy. I am free! I choose happiness and I choose freedom. I have made a choice (today) to forgive. Lord I'm ready to move into my future.

Amen.

13 EMBRACE AND EXTRACT

God sends people to us for various reasons. Sometimes we may be required to minister to them and other times they are sent to minister to us. Some are acquaintances, some friends, mentors or mentees. It is important to know a person's position in our lives but also be open to their counsel and advice.

We can learn something from each person that we connect with, even those that despise us.

Embrace who you are and who God is and extract from that goodness. Extract those things that will help you grow and realize that all things work together for your good, regardless of how they look. Even a seemingly bad situation can work for your good.

That doesn't mean *bad things* can't happen to *good people*. There are times in life when you are close to God, but you may still experience hardship. It is comforting that no matter what we may face in life, with God, we can conquer anything. We have hope with God as our Father.

Point

Love life and love others.

God came to give *all* hope. Your situation is never too *bad* nor too *big* for God.

As I have mentioned, mentors are important. Having trusted people to speak into our lives is valuable at every level. By embracing our mentors, we can extract what we specifically need. Embrace and extract. Extract those things that will make you a better person and help you to live a joyous life.

Learn from those God puts in your life, even if it is only for a particular time and season.

The embrace has to be mutual to be effective. You cannot help or be helped by someone that isn't ready for the embrace, let alone the extraction. My husband and I minister to countless people who are at different stages of life. There are times when we pour out and give direction and guidance, only to see and feel that it is being ignored.

It then becomes challenging to see someone go through something and know they aren't accepting what is being shared with them; it becomes a waste of time for both parties. When that happens, you must release that individual, because you cannot force anything that isn't accepted. Just think about our relationship with God; it is not forced but by free will that we follow Him. God doesn't want us to serve him out of force, but from open hearts that embrace His salvation and freedom.

ALL TALK AND NO RESPONSIBILITY

This generation seems to want to *talk it out* instead of *walk it out*. The "millennials" love advice, but upon receiving it they tend to do nothing with it. Counseling has become a new fad, and it's the "in" thing to do. I remember, back in the day, we had never heard of pre-marital (or any form) of counseling. Now it is popular. Ironically, we counsel before and during marriage, give advice and impart direction, but the divorce rate is still steadily increasing. My question is this: what are we doing with the advice given? Is the counsel that is given truly embraced? Or is it all a waste of time? Let's be clear I believe in counseling and I feel it can be effective if it is received. And not just received, but embraced and reacted upon.

In times past people prayed more than they talked. This generation wants to talk more than they pray. They in turn take no responsibility and shift the blame (on others or each other), for failure in their life and marriage. Everybody wants somebody to blame. Many blame their parents for their upbringing and all of the things they didn't receive as a child. Others blame their friends, spouses, their boss, coworkers, or the Pastor/Church for their failure. Some blame their Pastors, wife, Pastors family and their neighbors.

If their marriage is failing, they blame their spouse, or even the pastor for marrying them and not warning them about the pitfalls. What they fail to realize is that when they were asked by the Pastor if they were sure this was whom they wanted to marry, their response was, "Yes the Lord **told** me this was my mate," at which point, for most, the response must be, "Okay we can't argue with that". It then becomes "hands-off", because who can argue or refute what God says?

Point

Never place the blame on God for your decisions unless you are positive that it is God.

The way to cope with bad decisions that you have made is to embrace the fact that you made the bad decision and now you must face the consequences. It takes maturity to confess your faults and take responsibility for your life, and to receive Godly guidance and instruction as to how you should proceed.

TIME'S UP

There comes a time when you must realize when a person's season in your life is over. Let me clarify: of course marriage is long term, but some friendships and relationships will not last forever. As a matter of fact, no relationship will last forever, just as life here on earth will not last forever. We all know as Christians that eternal life is forever.

I can remember having intimate conversations with my children on this subject. My husband and I taught our children that they could befriend anyone and never limit themselves to one certain group of people.

We taught them to love people regardless of their culture, social status or race. With that, we also taught them to know when to draw the line, especially when it came to following the right path or going down the wrong road. We know that there are pitfalls in everyone's life. No matter how hard you try to stay on course, there will be ups and downs; peaks and valleys. The key is not to get "off track", and when you realize that you are headed in the wrong direction, navigate and get back on track. Reset and find your way back on the road to success.

Lower your expectations of people, because we are human. When expectations are lowered, we embrace the fact that we are owed nothing from anyone. Also, when you lower expectations, you will discover that you are less disappointed when people respond or act as you *feel* they should, because you never expected anything in the first place.

Point

Always remind yourself that within everyone is the
human element: the element to change.

With each passing day we are evolving, to hopefully become the person that God desires us to be.

Point

Times change and people change, but God never changes.

Lessons from Your Enemy

Open up your heart and know that you can learn valuable lessons from your enemy. I have learned a lot, not only from watching people, but also by taking to heart how I felt when placed in certain situations. I took lessons from my enemy. I would observe how they inflicted pain and hurt. I watched how they would talk about and hurt people with their venomous words.

I would come home from certain outside church functions as a Pastor's wife (after being verbally beat-up), and the first thing I would desire was to get all of our congregation in a room and hug every one of them. I wanted to assure them that Pastor and I love and cherish them unconditionally. I felt the need to let them know that they were appreciated. I had just left an environment in which I felt isolated and ignored. I knew that if I felt that way as the Pastor's wife, that someone in our congregation could be feeling the same way.

This was a defining moment that inspired me to go on a search and try and connect with those who felt alone. I know I couldn't physically reach everyone, but I would take time, get on the microphone and publically make my announcement of love. I always try to put myself in someone else's shoes. That is called empathy and it's something we all need more of. I extracted from the situation and embraced my instruction to respond by exemplifying love.

The heart of Jesus is big enough to embrace everyone, and whenever Jesus showed up on the scene, everyone extracted something from His life and the atmosphere. Those who heard that Jesus was near felt the need to get close to him because they felt that Jesus genuinely cared.

They embraced the love, hope and healing that only Jesus could give.

COPE AND STAY FOCUSED

There may be friends in your life now that may not be permitted to go into your future. Don't feel bad if one of your longtime friends no longer desires to be *friendly*. Be prepared to cope and stay focused. There are long-lasting friendships but there are also new friendships that will be birthed to help you reach your" God-given" potential.

If you are reading this book know that in order to effectively minister to others, you must make a personal decision to be whole and solid in your own character. Your Godly character will encourage you to see further than an individual's current state.

You are called to help others; you have to look beyond what you see and embrace the vision of whom God has called that individual to become. Everyone has those roller coaster moments when everything is up and down and sometimes around. Know that you are ministering to people who have the ability to change. By the same token, you are changing too. We all are a work in progress.

Here are a few notions my husband and I have extracted from our ministry through the years.

1. We do not own God's people

2. Our position in our congregation's life is to love them as Christ loves them— *unconditionally*. That means that when they come to our church, and even if they leave our church, love remains. We love them if they leave and if they return.

3. We recognize that some people are harder to love than others, but keep our hearts free of resentment and bitterness.

4. You are held accountable only for your actions. When you become hard and bitter toward others, it will rob you of your joy and possibly prevent future wholesome relationships. Never build up walls and categorize everyone as bad because of one person's evil actions.

5. Remember God has your back, front, sides and center. You don't have to watch your back, because God has your back! He will guard your heart, so don't hesitate to open it freely to love. Don't close yourself up or you will hinder growth and hinder new relationships. Know that as you draw close to God, He will draw nigh to you. God is the ultimate protector and guardian of your heart. You have nothing to fear.

6. Be happy and be free. Accept all of the goodness that God has reserved for you and know that your best days are ahead of you.

7. Learn to say "no" when necessary.

8. Don't stress over something you have no control over—give it to God. Remember that if you do worry you still have to give it to God.

9. Don't feel bad if you don't have solutions to everyone's problems. After you pray and give guidance or resources to help, it's up to the individual to implement and follow the plan.

10. I know that it is difficult to see those with a pure heart turn "bitter" because they are influenced by those who are bitter, tired and frustrated with life. Rest and know that you cannot protect them, they have to learn and remain strong when faced with disgruntled "mean"-spirited" people. Take the pressure off.

My mother told me growing up that you should never get so close to someone that you can't speak the truth. Allow space for human failure and realize that no one is perfect. We are all striving for perfection every day and with God we are becoming better each day. If you fall or make a mistake, don't stay down, get back up and move forward. Learn from your mistakes and vow never to fall prey to the same mistake twice.

My husband preached a life-changing message in which he enlightened our congregation to our spirits and how we are to guard them. He shared that our spirits are reserved for God and God alone. The moment you allow people to get into your spirit, they have crossed the line. Keep your spirit clear and full of the presence of God. Don't allow satan to cross jurisdictions and trespass into your spirit using people or the battlefield of your mind. Extract the bad and embrace the good. Speak up when necessary and guard your heart, ears and spirit.

11. Embrace God's glory as evidence that you have the ability to encourage and empower others, while demonstrating the power of unconditional love.

EXERCISE

Write Down Lessons learned from your enemy then apply them to your life.

_____

_____

_____

_____

_____

_____

_____

_____

_____

_____

_____

_____

_____

_____

_____

_____

_____

_____

_____

_____

_____

_____

_____

_____

_____

_____

_____

14 TRUTH VERSUS POP CULTURE

Pop culture: what's hot, what's popular. Truth, on the other hand, can be uncomfortable for some people. It can upset the popular *status quo* and make people angry.

When Jesus walked the earth, He was the embodiment of truth. Everywhere Jesus went there was a shake-up. His life was committed to speaking against tradition and religion God and He challenged things that were popular in that time, and remained steadfast in His mission. Jesus upset the religious leaders and their customs and because He was about His Father's business, and it made people uncomfortable.

The truth is still under attack, all these years later, and it is evident in the world. Look around and you will see the truth being challenged by disbelief and ridicule. The truth is being attacked in our government, community, homes, schools and places of worship.

We are quickly losing the true sense of family. We have compromised our morals and values, in lieu of wanting to make everybody feel okay with whatever they do, even if it is against God's word.

Who could have imagined a few years ago that the idea of a close-knit family would be viewed as fake or weird? Things are all confused these days.

HOME IS WHERE THE HEART WAS

What is "home"? Home should be a place of rest. A place where values are instilled and unconditional love flows freely. Back in the day, home was a place of shelter from the storms of life, and a place for family talks, shared meals, and peace. Home is where the heart was and a place of refuge and safety.

In today's culture, home has become a place of unrest, a place to run in, change your clothes and run back out. Now, in many cases, the more that people are away from home, the happier they seem.

Television and our mobile devices are now the babysitter, comforter and counselor. Uninterrupted verbal communication and "face-to-face" interactions are practically non-existent. Another casualty of our "have it now" society is our focus.

Some studies show that eight seconds is about all of the focus that this generation can muster. If we can't focus in for any amount of time, how can we spend quality time with those in our home? If our attention span is only eight seconds, which means that we are not focusing long on anything, which breeds frustration in not doing things quick enough. It makes me wonder, how can we process and retain information when we are moving rapidly? How can we feel peace and contentment when we are moving at such a fast pace?

Today's culture experiences less actual communication and more isolation. The truth is, we are meant to communicate with each other, especially our families. Communication within the family is critical. Pop culture is about the "express" in life and everything is "quick" and in a hurry. There is a definite lack of patience and this generation wants everything, NOW!

LET THE CHURCH SAY ("LIKE") AMEN

Church used to be the place where we gathered to learn more about God. It was absolutely imperative that we made it into God's house to receive wisdom and knowledge based on the word. Church is more than just a place to dress up for, socialize and "act" holy in. It is where we get our instruction and the weapons we need for the battles we fight every day of the week.

Many church communities are now nothing more than social gatherings. Preachers are afraid to speak truth for the fear that they may offend someone or lose members.

Hearing a "feel-good" message won't always get you to where you need to be in your life. We need to hear the truth!

Parents no longer insist that their children go to church. Children now tell parents whether or not they will attend church. When I grew up it was not an option. On Sunday morning we all went to church as a family. We are no longer raising our children under the fear and admonition of God and it seems as if children are controlling their parents. I can remember times being sick with stomachaches and, after telling my mom, she would say, "Get ready for church, the Lord is going to heal you today." Modern day parents seem afraid that if they reprimand their child, the child in turn won't like them. Parents of old could care less about being a child's best friend. As a matter of fact, they would tell them, "I am not your friend from the school, I am your parent." Now if a child tells their parents they are sick, the parent encourages them to stay home. The church was once viewed as a place from which we could receive help. The church was a place that we came to get it together; it was God's "hospital" for the saints.

MAKE CHURCH A PRIORITY

Church has always been and remains priority in my life. The very thought of not attending church on Sundays and Tuesdays seems awkward and weird. Church and the word of God is a very important part of my life.

So many parents now prioritize everything else in their children's lives over attending church. Extracurricular activities, basketball, football and ballet now take precedence over assembling ourselves in the house of God. I certainly understand balance and participation in activities outside of church, because the Shelby household was hopping, twenty-four-seven.

Ballet, basketball, football, student council, talent shows, piano lessons, trips to the library, gospel choir (I started a choir at the high school), field trips, plays, voice lessons, educational summits, art classes, birthday parties, honors assemblies, music group development and various after-school events were all a part of my children's life. That is just a partial list, to name a few of the things my children were involved in. We did it all and faithfully attended church services. With all of the activities, school and church, I asked God for *balance*. My husband and I decided that our desire was to develop well-balanced children that prioritized God first. We realized that if our children put God first then everything else in their life would fall into place.

My husband and I placed a family mandate in our home and discussed the importance of church attendance. We would allow our children (at a young age) to experience and hear the positives of why we should attend church services and participate.

It was important and we (my husband and I) committed to protecting our children from the stigma of the term "preacher's kids (PKs)". I have realized that there are certain heartaches that we as parents can protect our children from early on. We protect them through prayer, keeping their lives *balanced* and by covering them.

Attending church services for our family was the priority and many times I would let coaches know that my children may not be on time for a game, especially if it was on Sunday during service time. Our family would go to the games after church. Although the coaches may not have understood our decision, we really didn't let that bother us because we set the rules for our home.

Growing up, I can remember how we were taught to have respect not only for God's house but for the Sabbath day. It was so serious that we had church clothes, play clothes and school clothes. When we came back home from church we took our "church clothes" off and set them aside; they were for "church use" only. We even had "church shoes" and you didn't play in those shoes during the week. They were all for *church only*, and maybe a school play or a special event.

On Sundays, (after church) we would eat dinner as a family and this was a constant in our home. My mom wouldn't allow us to play outside on Sunday, as she felt that the Lord's day was sacred. This may have been extreme, and certainly we have evolved since then, but I believe that some of the same concepts of reverence and preparation for the house of God should remain as foundational teaching. My view of church and reverence helped me to honor and cherish the opportunity to be a part of a house of worship. I viewed my church as a place to receive instruction and strength to face the world and live a victorious life in Christ.

We must resume our position and recognize that we are the hands, feet and mouth of Jesus on the earth. If we don't share the un-compromised gospel, then what are we doing? As mentors and examples we must wake up and realize that only the word of God can equip, challenge and bring about change. Empowerment comes through the word and God and as we assemble ourselves we gain knowledge and strength. The word delivered by the Pastor or speaker equips everyone to live a victorious life.

I am amazed how some people never feel the necessity to come to the house of God, and question why should they attend services.

PASS OR FAIL

If you were to register for a college class and the professor explained that in order to pass the class you had to attend *every* class, you would comply and there would be no questions asked. We would feel that this was fair and that punishment for not doing so would be warranted. If we didn't honor the rules of the teacher, we wouldn't be surprised if we failed the class. As a matter of fact, we would predict failure and plan to either repeat the class, or enroll in another class. Think about the, if one decides to enroll in another class the same rules apply. Don't show up, don't do the necessary work and you will consequently fail.

The professor isn't necessarily trying to make things difficult for you, but they understand that the information that they need to impart is critical to your ability to pass the class. Dependent upon your educational goals, the professor knows that there must be an exchange and transfer of knowledge and information in order for you to be successful in your profession (after graduation). The professor has knowledge and has been positioned and contracted to share that knowledge, but he or she can't share if you don't show up for class.

How much more for the Pastor/Preacher and the house of God?

The Pastor has been mandated by God to impart wisdom, knowledge and the word of God to help you live an empowered and victorious life each time you leave the house of God. We assemble ourselves (in the house of God) to be replenished and receive a word that will help you live and fight the "good fight of faith" during the weeks, months and years to come. I believe that there are rewards given to those who not only have excellent attendance in the classroom, but excellent attendance in church as well. God gives out perfect attendance awards in more ways than you can imagine.

My Story

When my children were young, the Lord shared with me that the more I sat my children in his presence (at church), the more they would be shielded, equipped and protected. The Lord said that everything that I couldn't *give* or *do* for my children, by simply keeping them in the presence of God, He would fulfill. This holds true to everyone: the more you come into the presence of God (attend church regularly), the more God will bless you, simply because you place priority on what is most important…God.

Church is not about clubs, music, social gatherings, seeing your friends, having fun or programs. The church is about people, and equipping them for success in life. All of the other stuff might be fun and draw people to Christ, but it can't be the *main* thing. Souls are the reason why we exist and that's the bottom line.

Don't get it twisted. You need the word of God and you need to find a church home and Pastor that will love you and guide you into all truth. If you left the church, find your way back home. If you are sporadic in attending church, start attending church regularly.

FOUND IN AFRICA

I travelled to Africa on a mission and we had the chance to attend service and participate in a worship experience that drew more than 70,000 people who came from impoverished neighborhoods and had walked for miles to get to church. They piled into cars and excitement was in the air as they filled to capacity the stadium where the service was held. The worship experience lasted from 6:30pm to 6:30am the next day.

Hours and hours of the word of God, along with praise and worship, was the order of the night. They were so happy to come together in the presence of God, that neither time nor distance deterred them from getting there.

I think we are spoiled in this country. Our major concerns are focused more on the social aspects of church, and who we will see when we get there. Other areas that we overly concern ourselves with are what we wear, the entertainment aspect, and where are we going to eat after service.

People have lost focus of the *main thing*, and if service goes longer than expected, they complain and become impatient and bored.

Surprisingly those who feel that two hours is too long, are the same people that go to the mall and the movies the night before and will sit in a movie or shop for five hours with no problem. It is amazing to me that people can shop for six hours with no complaints, but when they get to church, they watch the clock and wonder how long it will take.

Satan has distracted us and made our own selfish pleasure the *main* thing, placing a spirit on people that makes them feel as if the house of God is boring and time consuming. It is the same spirit that makes reading a magazine exciting, but reading the Bible boring. Self-evaluate if when you read the newspaper you are alert, then when you start to read the bible you feel exhausted and sleepy. It is a spiritual attack to keep you locked out of opening the door to your knowledge (understanding), blessings and self-improvement. The Word of God is our *manual of success* and the promise, that holds the key and roadmap to unlock every blessing.

Remember, it is satan's desire to make church a miserable *secondary* experience and make worldly pleasures and carnality the priority. Don't be fooled by satan's devices which aim to keep you at a disadvantage spiritually. Let's be clear, I see nothing wrong with going to the movies or shopping, I personally enjoy both. But I know where my help comes from and where my priorities lie: in the house of God. If it's making a choice between going to a movie and going to church, I choose church, hands down!

SPOILED ROTTEN

If things aren't convenient we tend to want no part of it. The example that immediately comes to mind is of the service we attended in Africa. Many people of our congregation at home would have become hungry and bored, and would have walked out.

The people in Africa stayed in worship for hours on hard cement bleachers out in the open air with no concessions or other entertainment. I looked in awe and said that if an event of this magnitude had been held in the U.S., the response would have been totally different.

As a matter of fact, if we had to walk miles upon miles to get to church, so many wouldn't come. If we woke up on Sunday morning and had no electricity, many would not come to church. We complain about everything because life always has to be about convenience.

How far would you travel and what would you do to be able to experience God?

RESPECT

Generations and mindsets change, but truth never changes. When times change we need to build on a firm foundation of truth.

The modern attitude seems to be, "Do what you want" without conscience or consequence. Times have changed and the attack on this generation is great. We don't want to condemn anyone, but God's standards are immoveable. We can't settle for good enough. Good enough is the enemy of God's plan for your life. We are literally losing a generation because we don't take the time to listen to what God has to say.

Growing up, it was ingrained in me to respect the elderly and those in authority. At present common courtesy and respect are at an all-time low. As a child, I would tremble at the thought of disrespecting an adult. I knew what the consequence would be and that was enough to keep me on the straight and narrow path. It was called "fear".

This generation seems to fear no one. According to scripture, confidence and having no fear is a good thing, but there is no way around not instilling the fear of God in your children. How do you instill the fear of God?

Teach them to respect and honor God, the house of God, and God's people. Bring them to the house of God so that they can explore the word of God and learn good morals. Fellowship in the house of God is key, because it is where you and your children develop healthy friendships with those who believe as you believe.

Satan has instilled the fear in parents that if they bring their children to church too much they will fail in school and in the secular world. There is this new feeling that coming to church breeds failure. Satan has brought in a new ideology that if you really want to be successful and make it to the top, you should not be *too* "church going". This is a myth and farthest from the truth. It is just the opposite: without God, the church and a foundation, you fail.

Let's get back to setting a standard, representing God and redeveloping a kingdom mindset.

Of course there may be times that you have to miss church and certainly there are seasons where school activities, work or the like may be during service time, which is totally acceptable. My desire is to see everyone reach their fullest potential, and for those individuals that have an inward desire to be in God's house, God will always honor the heart of that individual.

SET A STANDARD

It is up to us as God's children to set a standard and teach the next generation. We can't teach them unless we are the example. Not to say anyone is perfect, but we must strive each day for perfection. My hope and prayer is to grow stronger each day and grow in understanding and wisdom.

COMMON SENSE: NOT SO COMMON

In this high tech age in which we live, it becomes easier to disconnect and replace verbal communication with texts, emails, and impersonal communication. Social media breeds a boldness that creates an environment in which anything goes and people feel they can or say or do anything they want.

Think about how many times people who would never be bold enough to say something critical to your face will log onto social media and be bold and malicious to you. They hide behind a screen and throw shade and in turn promote a spirit of disrespect.

It is only a coward who throws a rock and hides their hand. Stand up for the truth, even if it seems unpopular. Common sense and wisdom means… you don't share your intimate business with people you don't know or can't trust. I know you have accepted a lot of friends on social media, but also realize that some of your friends are enemies in disguise.

Social media has become a popularity contest and if you don't like someone's post they will hold it against you. You may not even be aware that you've hurt someone because you like another person's post and didn't like theirs. This is trivial, elementary school mayhem. You may use social media to run a business or promote ministry, and that's okay. Otherwise, successful people often don't have a lot of time for social media. If you find yourself on social media all day, make an effort to get off and do something more productive with your life, like read a book, visit someone in need, find a job or go back to school.

TIP

Never use social media to vent your frustration. It leaves the mind to wonder and brings a lot of innocent by-standers into your personal space. It creates confusion when you vent on social media and talk in riddles.

ACTION AND REACTION

We also need to know that every decision has consequences and every action causes a reaction.

Children have the right to express themselves online or in person, but they need to know that what they say or do can have a lasting effect, not only on others but on them. The wrong choice can cast a dark cloud over their future.

We approach decision making a lot differently when we recognize that for every decision there are consequences good or bad.

QUICK AND IN A HURRY

In modern day society, many simple arts are lost to the majority: arts such as cooking, cleaning, sewing, and playing an instrument are no longer deemed as important. This generation simply does not take time to sit down and learn such skills. Everything has to come quick. Young men no longer are interested in learning how to build a tree house, change the oil, wash the car, fix a flat tire or mow the lawn.

There is no more *balance* in life. The feeling exists that if I am domesticated then I can't pursue a professional career and education. This is furthest from the truth... Why not have it All!

Little girls no longer have a desire to play house and play with dolls. Little boys no longer are interested in playing with trucks and lawn mowers. Boys are no longer concerned with building a tree house with daddy or playing in the yard. Now modern day *boys* and *girls* want cell phones and video games. Although the *electronic age* has brought about great change and the ability to cause our children to process and think intelligently and technically...it has also robbed our children of the ability to cultivate and build what matters most... home, personal interaction, communication and character. It has robbed our children of common sense of how to think through the everyday things of life. Foundational principles, common sense and values should never be replaced. *Balance* is critical if we are to experience total self-fulfillment in real life. The ability to prioritize God, the Church, our homes and the ability to apply common sense will be the vital start to a" better "world.

The mentality is "I don't have to learn anything, if I need something done, I'll just pay someone else to do it."

What if you don't have extra money to pay someone?

This "get-rich-quick" mentality, means that this generation often fails to understand that it takes hard work, commitment and good stewardship to reach a certain financial status.

THE DARE DEVILS

A mentality of quick and easy success coupled with a deficit of common sense, breeds a fearless, dare devil attitude in a generation that feels it is *invincible*. The youth today rarely think of consequences or the fact that their choices are shaping their world.

Hypothetical: A young lady feels fearless and posts an inappropriate picture online. She doesn't realize at the time that, once posted, it could find its way into other people's hands and therefore never go away. As time goes on, she grows out of her mischievous ways and actually wants to get her life together. She graduates from college and applies for her dream job. Within the hiring process of this major corporation, the employer considers bringing her on board, but decides to do a little probing into her background. The employer goes onto her social media pages and finds pictures and posts that are a disgrace to what the company represents. The employer immediately comes to a decision not to hire her because of such inappropriate pictures and posts. The employer will never let her know the real reason for the decision not to hire her, but will call her back the next morning and say, "Sorry, we found someone that was more qualified for the position, we wish you the best."

This is real and happens every day in the corporate world.

Point

Watch what you do; no one is invincible. There are consequences to every action, whether good or bad.

FINAL AUTHORITY

Parents are the final authority in the home. The Bible says:

> Train up a child in the way he should go: and when he is old, he will not depart from it. (Proverbs 22:6 KJV)

We should always know what our children (as minors) are doing online: in particular, who they are talking to and who they are meeting. No parent should be locked out of a child's life, on or offline. Stay current and connected and keep the communication lines open. Teach your children all that you can before the world teaches them different.

Even with mine and my hubby's desire to teach our children everything, I admit there were times in life that I scratched my head and said, "How did I miss that? Lord, if I could go back, I would have told them about that!"

Times are constantly changing and as parents we may not get it all in, but that's where trust and independence has to come into play. We know that God has to do the rest. God is the final authority over everything and everyone.

Point

We train up our children in the way that they should go and as parents God had given as promise …when they grow old, they will not depart.

MY STORY,
PART TEN
SWEET SIXTEEN

Back in my day, the church frowned upon wearing make-up and "painting your face". We were only allowed to wear petroleum jelly on our lips and if you wanted anything else, that was not going to happen. I have no regrets because I have embraced my upbringing and that was what God ordered for my life; it kept me walking the straight and narrow.

But when I had girls, I personally wanted to do things a little differently as times were different. There was a part of me that wished I'd had someone in my youth to invest in my appearance and show me what was current and how to develop a beauty regime that would enhance my beauty. That is what I taught my girls, that when you apply makeup, it should only enhance your natural beauty.

I also used the platform of makeup, facial cleansing and body care to talk with them about inner beauty and how above all God desires that we place emphasis on our spiritual care.

I did not want my daughters discovering makeup as late in life as I did, nor did I want someone else teaching them about those important things teenagers must learn, so I took the time to show them everything I wasn't shown as a teenager. At that time, it was enough for my mom to tell me, "Live Holy", and "Love God"; she didn't have to go into detail about much more. I watched her life and how she loved God and emulated it.

The current generation has become a lot wiser and they not only want to hear, "Live Holy", they want to know how. If we are to reach this generation, we have to prepare ourselves to give honest instruction and answers, to make sure that our children receive the example, wisdom and knowledge to make this world better. After all, every generation should be wiser. That should be every parent's dream.

SWEET SIXTEEN

When my girls reached the sweet age of sixteen, my husband took each of them out on their first date. They would dress to the nines (he in a tux and she in a formal dress), and he would make reservations at a five-star-restaurant, pick them up from the house and take them out for the evening.

It was a teachable moment, as he was showing our daughters how a gentleman was to treat a lady and setting a standard.

Complete with roses and chocolate, Don would have a long conversation with them about dating etiquette, relationships and our expectations.

At the end of dinner, Hubby gave each of them a gold and diamond heart, which would be a symbol of our desire for them to remain close to their mommy and daddy's hearts, and to remain sexually pure until marriage. This has been a tradition in the Shelby household, and I pray that it will be passed on to future generations.

Point

Talk with your children about life and not only
tell them, but teach them by example.

Take the Pressure Off

This is for every parent with great expectations for their children: Never fail to express your expectations to your children.

Once you share them, live your life to the best of your ability in order to be the example that they can follow. The standards that you hold for your children and others should be the same as those for your own personal life. Actually, the bar should be higher, because you should *do* and *be* the best of what you expect of others.

This doesn't mean that you will never make a mistake, because you will, but you should be transparent enough to share those mistakes at the appropriate time. It doesn't take anything away from you to say to your child that you have made a mistake and you're sorry.

Your transparency may prevent them from going down the same path. Take the pressure off of being perfect! That is a healthy way to raise your children, by letting them know that nobody's perfect! There is only one that is perfect, and that is Jesus Christ. Each day we strive for perfection in His example. Life is full of people with imperfections, but with Christ in our lives, we never stop growing and working on ourselves.

Again realize that although the Bible tells us to "train up a child in the way [they] should go" (Proverbs 22:6 KJV), that is not to say that we can prevent our children from never making a bad decision. They will. As a parent, you just have to make sure you do your part, because when you instill truth and clear expectations, the word of God says they "will not depart." This means that if they choose another path, they are still protected with the knowledge of truth. When we teach and impart wisdom, and the love of God, we are giving this generation, as well as future generations, a priceless gift.

EXERCISE
START A LEGACY

Start a family tradition and keep open lines of communication. Promote verbal communication and a close-knit relationship with your children and spouse or loved ones.

Think of a family tradition that you can start today. Write a few ideas here and put them into action

_____

_____

_____

_____

_____

_____

_____

_____

_____

_____

_____

_____

_____

_____

_____

_____

_____

_____

_____

IT'S A NEW DAY

There are certain laws in place right now that protect your child's privacy. It doesn't matter how much a parent protests, when your child reaches a certain age, they have a right to withhold information from you regarding their personal lives. There is a part of your child's life that you may never know about, and information that you will never be privy to. That's why it is important that you do your part at home. Open dialogue with the children, teach them and stress open communication at a young age. Let them know that you realize they may not always tell you everything, but that you are open to listening and that you will love them unconditionally, no matter what they *say* or *do*.

Keep your children in church and in the presence of God so that they will embrace honesty with a pure heart and a desire to stand firm in living a *good* life. Again, God promised that by keeping my children in His presence, He would supply anything that I could not give. Communicate vision, pray, and stay connected as parents.

MY STORY, PART ELEVEN THE CHECK-UP

When my daughter Amber went to the doctor for a checkup at age seventeen, the medical staff asked me to leave the room. They informed me of a new policy that stated parents of children age sixteen and above have to leave the room when their child is being examined. This policy also included asking the child if they are comfortable with their parent being in the room while they take their vitals.

I was in shock and Amber, too, saying "Mommy you can stay in here."

The nurse said, "No, we are sorry, Amber, this is policy. Mom will be back after we finish."

"Wow, times have changed," I thought to myself. I peacefully left the room and sat in the waiting room, a little bit upset. "Huh, this is my baby and after all I went through to have her they have the nerve to ask me to leave the room?"

I picked up a magazine and began to turn the pages pretty hard until the small voice said, "It's okay, and it's the policy, not just for you but for everyone. You will be back in the room in a minute. Calm down, Bonita."

I listened and calmed down immediately. (I was reminded by the still small voice of my own rule- "stop, shut up, and listen")

I thought about how we'd kept open the lines of communication with our children and I knew I had taken care of them and that there was nothing to worry about.

As parents, we all know that our children will not always talk to you about everything, but at least they should know that mom and dad are there to listen and love them, regardless of what they go through. Love is the standard, regardless. Although we may be disappointed in a decision or a choice that they have made, we will never stop being parents and loving our children unconditionally. I found peace in the waiting room and the pages of the magazine were now turning at a much calmer pace.

After twenty minutes the nurse came out and said, "Mrs. Shelby, you can come back now."

I said "Yay!"

The doctor then explained the new policy and that it was to protect the privacy of teenagers and children that may be experiencing abuse or hardship in their home or within themselves. I nodded my head to signify that I understood. I was still a little upset.

The doctor then stood up and said, "Mrs. Shelby, you and your husband are wonderful parents, and you have done an amazing job raising your daughter Amber. I commend you as parents, Amber is an awesome young lady, destined for great things."

I looked at her in wonder and said, "So, you took me out of the room to ask her questions that I couldn't hear, only to tell me I did a great job as a parent?"

NO WAY

When Amber and I were on the way home, she told me all of the routine questions the doctor asked.

Doctor: Are you using drugs?

Amber: No way!

Doctor: Your mom and dad don't have to know, but are you sexually active?

Amber: No way!

Doctor: Are your parents abusing you?

Amber (becoming even more aggravated): No Way.

Doctor: Is there was anything you want to talk to me about that you don't feel comfortable talking to your parents about?

Amber: No, I can talk to my parents about anything

Wow, this is what the world is coming to! I had to think that this may have been put in place and necessary for that poor child that suffers abuse and has no one to care for or protect them.

Of course what they didn't know is that as soon as Amber got into the car, she was upset by my exclusion from the room and the questions that she felt were odd and offensive. I explained it to the best of my ability. Amber listened to my explanation and nodded her head reluctantly to affirm.

I am thankful that Amber has a desire to please God and she knows her foundational beliefs, how much her parents love her and that, with God, her life can be built on a firm foundation.

A FIRM FOUNDATION CAN'T BE EASILY SHAKEN.

There is one foundation upon which we must build: *Truth*. The moment we embrace *truth*, we must teach to the upcoming generations the importance of building their lives upon the principle of honesty and integrity. Honesty begins with an inward will to embrace our beliefs and stand by them without wavering. Everyone has the ability to choose what he or she believes and I am convinced that a firm foundation begins with biblical principle. When we honor and revere God it will encourage us to change for the better. By changing ourselves, we can impact the world in which we live.

15 MY SECRET WEAPON

Ye are of God, little children, and have overcome them: because greater is he that is in you, than he that is in the world. (1 John 4:4 KJV)

(For the weapons of our warfare are not carnal, but mighty through God to the pulling down of strong holds;) (Corinthians 10:4 KJV)

Point

You have a secret weapon.

With God in your life you have the edge. With each day, you have a brand new opportunity to fulfill every goal and dream. It's time to reach the target!

Love life itself and with each day will come a new opportunity to fulfill your dreams.

Your secret weapons are God, praise, character and confidence.

PRAISE

Praise is your weapon. When you activate it, you can change and destroy the tactics of the enemy. When you praise God, you actually take control of the situation and counteract the bad. Praise will spring up and invite the presence and power of God to inhabit every situation, good and bad. God inhabits the praise of His people. When praises go up, blessings come down. Praise shatters the heavens and releases the *divine* in your life.

Praise also confuses the enemy. Satan wonders, "How can they still adore and honor God when everything is going haywire?"

Right here in the middle of this chapter, take a moment and praise and admire God for who God is, what God has done, and what God is doing in your life right now. Your blessing is coming down the pipeline. Expect the divine and the supernatural!

GODLY CHARACTER

Godly character will preserve you and sustain you along your journey. Work daily on your relationship with God. Traits of Godly character are; evident when we live a life of truth, honor, integrity and respect. Great character is the ability to treat other people the way you want to be treated. Love is also key: love covers and protects. Love sees the best before the worst and understands that there is hope. God is *love* and if you have God in your life and honor Him then you will have *love* in your heart.

Point

God is Love…Got God?... Got Love. No God?.......No Love.

Confidence

When you are confident in who you are in God, you will walk with *authority*. As you grow, you will begin to understand your right as a "child of the King" who has created all things as well as the universe. You will enter into a place of satisfaction in being *uniquely* and *unapologetically* you. Make up your mind to walk into your God-ordained destiny, continually in pursuit of becoming exactly who God has intended you to be. You are great because your Father is great and God has invested so much in you.

> **Point**
>
> Love yourself the way God loves you—unconditionally. Learn to measure up to your own expectations and, not anyone else's.

My personal goal is to give my all as I embark upon the fulfillment of my dreams. It took a while, but I came to the conclusion that I won't sell myself short when I know I have heard from God. Outward beauty is skin deep, and it is the *inner* struggle that many deal with every day. Many battle each day with the guilt of their past and the consciousness of their sins. Everyone is in constant warfare between the flesh and the sprit. We fight against time and recognize that yesterday is gone and will not return, but with God and hope, tomorrow is not lost.

Everything is in God's time, and in order to fulfill our destiny, we must pull out our *secret weapon*. No longer allow the fear of a failure, nor the guilt of your past to hold you hostage. Free yourself and loosen every chain that ties you within the confines of your own mind and strips you of your confidence. No longer second-guess God. Know what God says, then respond. Remember, satan will constantly remind you of your dark past and use others at the moment that you feel you have finally made it to the place of forgiving yourself and others. Satan is an accuser and will send someone to remind you of your past. His motive is to keep you off balance and bitter. As satan reminds you of your past you remind him of your future.

A bitter and imbalanced individual lies down at night frustrated with the day and then wakes up in the morning just as frustrated and negative, not only towards themselves, but towards everyone else. They want to make everyone pay for their misery. They are bitter from past hurt, rejection and pain. They have fortified walls that they have built against others and they trust no one.

THE "OPPOSERS"

When an individual carries the presence and glory of God in their lives, face it ...they will automatically offend others. It is the anointing on your life that causes others to dislike you. The funny thing is, you are not trying to offend, but when you exemplify the love of Christ, it is offensive to those in darkness. Remember: When light comes forth, darkness has to flee. The satanically motivated hatred of others tries to overpower the intent of your heart and make you weary and depressed. Come out of your depression and weariness now. Satan is defeated!

Everywhere Jesus went, he brought about change and a buzz about town. When the town found out that Jesus was near they would follow him in search of their miracle and the undeniable presence of God.

That made others mad, because they wanted to know what it was about Jesus that caused such a stir. The anointing breeds success, and the enemy will constantly try to keep tabs on you and despise you because they can't figure out why you are so successful. They know that they have done everything to hinder your success by slandering your name, blocking your progress and trying to spread hatred, yet you are still favored. When people call your name too much, jealousy will arise in others and the spirit of Saul will be in them.

The "opposers" will hate you for your success, but do not find yourself apologizing or dumbing yourself down! Your main concern should not be to try to fit in with such people. Their hate may cause you to lose focus of your mission and mandate.

Realize that your enemy is sent to destroy you, to make you give up! The devil will use people and the battlefield of your mind to cause you to feel incapable and lose your confidence. That's where depression takes over from the joy and happiness of serving God.

Shake off your enemy and stay focused. The time has come for you to be everything that God has called you to be. Your destiny awaits . . . there is no time to lose. Continue to give glory back to God where it belongs. The anointing will always give you the edge and keep you a step ahead of your haters.

Remember that, when an individual is not happy with themselves, it manifests in hatred towards others—even the innocent. Again, "hurting" people in turn" hurt" people.

It doesn't matter what people say about you, it is all about how you define yourself. Ladies, pull out your secret weapon of Godly confidence. Know *who* and *whose* you are. You were created in God's image. You will turn heads because with God on the inside you are beautiful. Don't measure your beauty by your size, a hairstyle or a designer dress. Don't measure your self-worth by the opinions of others. Measure you by God and yourself.

Define your successes and personal victories. Let praise, your love for God, and your love for who God has made *you* be your secret weapon. If you are overcome with jealousy and hatred because of someone else's success, I implore you to ask God to give you a *pure heart* towards others. Jealousy will always keep you at a disadvantage. Enjoy life, celebrate you and learn to celebrate someone else as well!

MY STORY,
PART TWELVE
MY SECRET
WEAPON
REVEALED

In chapter 6 I spoke a little bit about an uphill journey. In this chapter I'll reference it again because it was the year that I embraced my secret weapon: my "Forty and Fabulous" experience with God.

I remember it like it was yesterday. One a Sunday after service I went to my office to place a phone call. I sat down at my desk and God began to minister to my spirit. The coming week I would celebrate my fortieth birthday. I had been reflecting on my life, and that's when revelation came.

Many women feel that after forty, it's "downhill". Of course, the body goes through changes, both mentally and physically. But my question is this: Why accept a downhill journey?

Why do women get depressed in their old age? Take your measure and work it out. Embrace your age. Don't lie or deny. The more you embrace it, the longer life God can give. I have never and will never be ashamed to tell my age. It is by the grace of God that I have lived this long. I gladly share my age and I have noticed that individuals who speak truth concerning their age and they are thankful, they tend to enjoy life and in most cases (there are exceptions) live longer/productive lives. They are not in a fight to stay young, but they enjoy life and the aging process. They are not in a battle or competition with life and longevity, but they embrace each day given as precious. In other words, they are not fantasizing or working hard to prove they are young, they cherish living life in their lane and thankful for where they have been and where they are going.

On my fortieth birthday, the Lord came and said, "Get ready to live your uphill journey! No more wondering in the wilderness."

Canaan land. I knew my later journey through life would be even greater than my former.

I'm on an *uphill journey* on my way to heaven. Don't trip, now I am going nowhere anytime soon but that day pressure was lifted. No longer would I exert all of my energies trying to please people. Everybody is not going to like you, but for every one that doesn't like you, there are *twenty* that love you. Count your losses and surround yourself with those who genuinely care and appreciate who you are.

It would blow my mind how, after starring in a reality television show, I would be walking down a hallway, or need assistance, and I would be ignored. But as soon as people discovered that I had been on a national television show they would all of a sudden roll out the red carpet. My response was, "Wait a minute, I'm the same person that you just blew off and treated poorly—the same person you just rolled your eyes at!"

Don't be fake, people; treat everybody right.

My hubby always teaches our congregation to treat everyone like a VIP, including the children. Treat everyone as you would want to be treated. Ladies, stop wasting valuable time and energy being petty with and about one another. Protect your sister and be bold, brave and mature enough to speak up for one another. Don't be a coward; if you need to know something or have a question for your sister about her actions, ask her. Don't ask around.

Women have a way of being petty and subtle enemies. They will do conniving little things to shut each other down. Example, they will smile and act as if they adore the ground you walk on, then as soon as you get up on stage (or otherwise) to do something, they get up like clockwork, claim to be busy and walk out. They can't stand to hear you speak, neither can they stand to hear anyone compliment or celebrate you. If this is you ...stop the jealousy and the foolishness and ask God to purify your heart. Why hate (or become jealous of) your sister because she is successful, celebrated, and loved? This makes no sense. It absolutely makes no sense when women become aggravated if another woman's husband adores and celebrates her. You should be happy for your sister and certainly if you are single you should pray that God gives you a spouse that celebrates you as well. Many people are at a disadvantage. They are not prosperous and blessed because they hate instead of celebrate. It's time for a Heart check!!!

Let's be honest, loving and mature. You only hinder yourself when you criticize, tear down or ignore others to build yourself up.

At forty I said, "I'll cut my losses." I became confident, and now I know when to let go!

Ladies, we are on an uphill journey; embrace it now! No more "Lordy, I'm forty" depression. You only get better!

THE UPHILL JOURNEY: MY CONVERSATION WITH GOD

You may ask, what is an uphill journey?

It is one where you:

- Remain focused on your destiny
- Don't allow people to dictate your happiness
- Other people's opinions don't matter when it comes to fulfilling God's purpose
- Know that you are fearfully and wonderfully made
- Strengthen your relationship with God daily
- Recognize that your sole mission should be to pour into and empower others
- Grow wiser and stronger every day
- Take your challenges and turn them into triumphs
- Become strong, and resilient
- Don't fight battles that bring you no spoils
- Put your hope and confidence in God and no one else.
- Lower your expectations of people
- Celebrate others and free yourself of jealousy and hatred

- Don't accept that you are going downhill with age

What should have taken the children of Israel less time took forty years of wandering. I want to prevent and safeguard this generation from the forty-year wilderness by saying: Follow God's plan and where there are no shortcuts the Promised Land is nigh, as long as you navigate according to God's plan.

The process of getting better never ends in a relationship. When you invest and are confident in who you are, you can keep on getting better. Your "better" is strictly for you and fulfilling your purpose in the Kingdom.

After you have made an investment in yourself, you won't be intimidated by any other beautiful woman. They may look different than you, seem smarter, and even appear to have more, but, when you realize your only competition is with yourself, it takes the pressure off. There is always going to be someone out there that may look better, but realize that you have nothing to be intimidated by or worried about.

Point

Your secret weapon is your unique ability to exclusively be yourself.

The Secret Weapon of Confidence

Living a confident life is key. I encourage everyone who reads this book to work on your confidence and know your purpose and self-worth. It is important that you seek God for your purpose and recognize that you were placed here on earth to make a difference. Your purpose is not one of defeat but you are a conqueror. You can conquer anything with God in your life.

Confidence comes when you recognize that your sufficiency is only through living a victorious God-directed life. There may be times of suffering or trial but God will give us the strength to endure all hardship and pain.

> 35. Cast not away therefore your confidence, which hath great recompense of reward.
>
> (Hebrews 10:35 KJV)

Never throw away your confidence, it is a key weapon to gain your victory. As the scripture says, don't cast it away because if you can hold on to it, there is a great reward.

The pressures of life come to strip you of your confidence to excel and succeed. Speak with authority and believe what God has prepared and declared over your life. Be strong in the Lord and in the power of *His* might. That means that times when you feel weak and incapable, know that with God you can do anything. Start by speaking the victory until you begin to experience and see victory. Why Not Have It All?

THE CONFIDENT WIFE

> Whoso findeth a wife findeth a good thing, and obtaineth favour of the LORD.
>
> (Proverbs 18:22 KJV)

Wives when your husband married you, he obtained favor. Know that you have what it takes to be everything that your husband needs, wants or desires. Trust in God and be confident in yourself.

As a "good thing" (a wife) there is a secret weapon of confidence that you should embrace.

You are the *good* that is specifically designed for your mate. You don't have to look over your shoulder to see if another woman is *eyeing* your man because, first of all, if your husband is strongly committed to God, you can trust the God in him. Your job is to give your all and continually be that "good thing" to him in return. If someone can step up and take him away after you have done your absolute best, then he is not the godly man you deserve.

SINGLE LADIES WALK IN CONFIDENCE!

Remain confident in that just because you are single it does not mean that you are alone. You are *not* lacking *anything* when you follow the plan of God for your life. Never compare your life to others and begin to move at your own "God-ordained" pace. You have the secret weapon of confidence that says "I am whole and entire". "I won't settle". "I want God's absolute best!"

Confidence in God during your "single life" is key so that you won't fall prey to the trap of *vulnerability*. The moment you become vulnerable, will be the opportunity for the wrong person to take advantage of you. Vulnerability will open you up to the tricks and traps of satan. That's why it is imperative that you embrace your "singleness" and embrace God as "Jehovah Jireh" (your provider.)

Stay clear of adulterous relationships and remember married men are off limits! Don't set your life up for failure and reap the consequence of bad behavior by feeling it is okay to date or entertain married men. Your purpose in life is not to gain the reputation of a "side chick". You are better than that. Don't allow men to play games with you an fill your head with lies, that his plan is to divorce his wife and walk away from his family to be with you. For most single ladies that is a promise that most men won't keep but they will put your life on hold because deep down they want to have the best of "both worlds". Life then becomes one of broken, unfulfilled promises and eventually will lead to depression, and low self-worth. In previous chapters, I spoke of an important word that will keep you grounded in making good choices...*empathy*. How would you feel as a wife and mother if you experienced infidelity? Think about the consequences. Gods law of reciprocity is real. You will reap what you sow.

Single ladies realize that God has a wonderful plan for your life and if you can exercise patience and confidence…you will walk in your promise and reach your destiny. God's plan for your life is not that you are vulnerable and naive. Your name is not, "easy", "silly" or "home wrecker." Cherish the scripture of a "good name " and that it is better than riches.

Don't hold your breath waiting on Mr. Right, pursue your goals and live your dream. Confidence says if I am waiting there must be a just cause. Ask God to fill every void of loneliness while you wait and "shut the noise" on the negative voice that says that your biological clock is ticking away and you don't have much time left.

God is working on you every day and preparing you to become the wife, and mother that He desires. You are whole and entire.

Point

In order to be found, you have to get lost! Get lost in God's love and
He will fill you up, so that you won't have room for anything else.

Point

While single allow God to fill every void in your life

> **Point**
>
> God will keep you if you desire to be kept

It is harder to hold on than it is to let go. **Keep holding on!**

THE PRESENCE OF GOD IN ME

Ladies, take time to invest in your happiness. The key is to make a choice to be happy. Self-defeat is real and yes, there is a battle going on in our minds. Remember you have a secret weapon that you can work to find: your confidence.

> **Point**
>
> Don't turn on yourself—you are all you've got! God made you an original, so don't live life like a "knock off."

There is no replica of you on earth. Realize that God is counting on you to fulfill your purpose and pursue your destiny. No one else on the planet can accomplish the purpose you were put on earth for. Walk boldly in your authority and don't offer any apologies for who you are or what you have accomplished. Give glory to the one who enabled you to soar, and give back to those who are under-privileged. Never forget the wonderful wisdom you have acquired along life's journey. When you become whole and allow God to heal you, you will be able to help, heal and deliver others.

Keep your *arsenal* packed and know that your secret weapon is . . . you! You are a threat to the devil and you have already been equipped to defeat *every* enemy.

16

THE VICTORY RIGHT WHERE YOU ARE

I've got the victory and my story has a happy ending. Your story is one of victory and success. You are a survivor. Embrace you, love life and use the practical things in this book to bring balance to your life.

God wants you to have victory, right where you are. Your blessings are going to begin to chase you down and overtake you. Long-awaited miracles and the ability to call blessings into motion are within your grasp.

You have the power to overcome the obstacles and problems that distract you and throw you off balance from your purpose. God is bringing balance to your life and preparing you for your promise! Why Not Have It All?

I am blessed, but there have been times when I couldn't see my way and God made a way of escape. He did it for me and He is going to do it for you!

You learn from mistakes and your problems teach you how to strategize and strengthen your relationship with God. Your testimony of victory is being written right now. According to God's plan and promise, trials were not meant to destroy you, but to make you stronger. From every mistake and circumstance, learn to extract strength and stamina and be the *amazing* person God created you to be. You are a success story! You can have it all! The Choice is Yours!

EXERCISE

A. Write down areas of your life in which you are victorious

B. If you were given one key to unlock a treasure in your life, what would that treasure be?

_____

_____

_____

_____

_____

_____

_____

_____

_____

_____

_____

_____

_____

_____

_____

_____

_____

_____

_____

_____

_____

_____

17 THE CHECKLIST ☑

Consider these affirmations and how you will implement changes that can make these statements true to you.

- ☐ I win -I'm a survivor
- ☐ I view life through a positive Lens-God can turn negatives into positives
- ☐ I love God and I accept Jesus as my Lord and Savior
- ☐ I am beautiful
- ☐ I will perfect and live a blessed and *balanced* life
- ☐ I choose to be happy
- ☐ I will work on gaining more wisdom and knowledge
- ☐ I am intelligent
- ☐ I am prosperous
- ☐ I view my challenges as set-ups and possibilities
- ☐ I believe in the supernatural
- ☐ I will give God time each day through consecration and devotion
- ☐ I will take out time to find a church home and attend services regularly
- ☐ I will pray more and talk less
- ☐ I am Prosperous-wealthy in many ways
- ☐ I will make my contribution to this world- I will think of something none has thought of, or invent something that has *never* been invented
- ☐ I will be considerate of others feelings-empathy
- ☐ I am a conqueror
- ☐ I am not Alone-God is always there.
- ☐ I am Kingdom Minded
- ☐ I am an ambassador for Christ - I am his feet, hands and mouth in the earth. I will represent well
- ☐ I will take valuable "me "time.
- ☐ I will fulfill all of my dreams
- ☐ I will explore new ways to bring **balance** to my life
- ☐ I will bring order to everything in my life that is unorganized
- ☐ I will succeed at everything that aligns with God's will for my life.
- ☐ I will pray for others-

- ☐ God has great plans for my life
- ☐ My ability to learn and gain more knowledge is important to my overall success
- ☐ My confidence is the key to my Success-I know who I am
- ☐ I will make good choices as I listen to the voice of God
- ☐ I will work hard to establish a strong moral foundation
- ☐ I will quiet myself when necessary-and speak out when necessary
- ☐ I will recommit to my marriage (if married)
- ☐ My marriage is a direct reflection of the love of God (if married or desire marriage)
- ☐ I will strive to be a lovable person -I will open up my heart to love and be loved
- ☐ I am happy to see other people blessed
- ☐ I will not live my life as a victim
- ☐ I am not a loner and I will not live in isolation
- ☐ I am Free
- ☐ I am content
- ☐ I will accept my assignment of mother (lioness) to my biological and spiritual children
- ☐ I am strong and courageous
- ☐ I choose to forgive
- ☐ I will open up my heart and embrace God's will for my life
- ☐ I will extract and embrace God's goodness and mercy
- ☐ I need a mentor
- ☐ I will not fail
- ☐ I am a leader
- ☐ I will build on a firm Foundation-Jesus Christ
- ☐ I have the victory
- ☐ I deserve God's best
- ☐ I am on schedule for my "BIG BREAK"
- ☐ I can have it ALL!

You may ask **"Can I Really Have It All?**

My response, **"Why Not?" "Yes You Can!"**

THE ONE AND ONLY YOU!

This book is dedicated to you! It is important that you make every day count and that you take care of yourself.

- Keep stress levels to a minimum

- Get plenty of rest

- Change up your routine-shake life up!

- Make life exciting-take a different route to work

- Eat properly

- Drink plenty of fluids

- Schedule regular checkups

- Find a place of worship

- Pray. It is essential and your communication with God is imperative

- Schedule "Me Time "that is time that is dedicated to making yourself happy. Tea time, a candy bar, reading a good book, going to the spa or taking a much needed nap.

- Start a prayer journal

- Exercise regularly (consult with your physician)

- Read **"Why Not Have It All",** more than once and share with friends.

Final Point

Stay in touch with God and stay tuned, because God is doing great things in your life!

Why Not Have It All! ~Bonita Andrea Shelby

NOTE FROM THE AUTHOR BONITA ANDREA SHELBY

This book entitled, **"Why Not Have It All"**, will change your life and open up your understanding to the meaning of true self-fulfillment. We have explored the term "balance", its importance and offered practical advice on how to achieve your personal dreams and aspirations...and help others to do the same. The purpose of the book is to minister not only to women, but anyone that has a desire to live a full and free "balanced" life.

As you read, **"Why Not Have It All"**, you will be encouraged to write, think and develop your plan and soar. "Why Not Have It All", is a book that encourages the reader to create and see results through practical knowledge, my life experiences as well as scripture references.

Apply what is learned and execute a plan that will yield success. God is counting on you to make a great impact in the world, and I am routing on you to succeed. I commit to praying for you and as you read, extract that which applies to your life. Make great choices, share wisdom **and Live Well!** God has ordained the strategy to "great" success, so take your ***key and unlock your hidden treasure***. You are a *success story* and *you win*!

CPSIA information can be obtained
at www.ICGtesting.com
Printed in the USA
BVOW04*1825100417
480855BV00009B/18/P